This book is being given to

_____

because I care about you.

_____

[Affix business card here]

What Life Insurance Agents Are Saying about *The Secret Asset*

"Powerful mathematics! A new take on the real math behind life insurance and why it should hold a place in everyone's diversified portfolio. A common-sense story that my clients can understand and a great gift for all my clients in the medical field."

Dan Yacker

"David puts the 'life' back in life insurance. Wow!"

Lee Goldsmith

"This strategy is fantastic. D'Arcangelo takes away the mystery behind all those hard-to-understand life insurance illustrations. Why wouldn't you buy as much life insurance as possible at net-zero cost when you can potentially yield IRRs far in excess of almost any other asset class?"

Mike Knowles

"This book provides excellent insights and strategies into the often overlooked asset David calls 'investment-grade life insurance.' I'll be keeping this book on my desk so I can make it a part of my clients' investment planning conversations!"

Michael C. Holt

"This book opens up new strategies and ideas that have been extremely successful. I recommend this book for insurance agents and their clients."

Kyle Perkins

"Investment-grade life insurance should be in every qualified family's portfolio. As one of my clients said when he realized the true value of life insurance, 'There is no risk that my family will receive a seven-figure tax-free payoff on my policy that will beat the return on most every position in my financial portfolio. It's just a matter of when they will receive the check.'"

Brian Menendez

"The truth about life insurance has been too obscure for too long. David's telling of the tales reveals the underlying strength of life insurance as an available asset. Opening your mind to these opportunities and taking the time to understand the power in the numbers will reward those who employ David's strategies."

John W. Cochran, Jr.

"Finally, someone makes it easy to understand. This is by far the best insurance guide I have ever read. I plan on giving each one of my clients a copy."

Edward L. DeWitt

"David, in the subtlest of ways, makes understanding the intricacies of life insurance elementary yet intriguing at the same time. His idea to create and paint a picture of a family's needs is ingenious, and it is something I will definitely share with clients."

Shane Walton

What Consumers Are Saying about *The Secret Asset*

"Clinging to old beliefs in these uncertain times is a recipe for disaster. Thankfully, David D'Arcangelo has written another paradigm-shattering book that shows you exactly how to profit from one of the simplest, yet most misunderstood, financial tools available. Read this book and change the financial future of your family for generations to come."

Robert Helms, Host, *The Real Estate Guys*

"Wow, David once again shares with us not only his wisdom concerning the big picture of one's financial landscape, but also a way in which to live a value-driven life financially. David's strategies and thinking can change our children's lives as well as those charities that will be sustained even after we have passed on. Thank you, David!"

Susan Wheeler, Real Estate Loan Consultant

"David D'Arcangelo is a financial and insurance genius. He has helped many people make money in low-risk life insurance. In this book, he has clearly presented another great opportunity to make money with investment-grade life insurance. The policy will result in high returns at a tax-free rate."

Robert Nakamura, M.D.

"This book has managed to translate complex financial strategies so that anyone can benefit from wealth management techniques that have previously been available only to the wealthiest families. These strategies are brilliant. Inside these pages, I found many other valuable lessons that are, quite literally, priceless."

Michael Teitleman, Retired Headmaster, The Bishops School

"This book makes an excellent case for investment-grade life insurance. It very much reminds me of several monographs I read in the 1960–1975 period that venture capital investments were becoming worthy of serious consideration by institutional investors. At this time, VC was considered a special cult area exclusively populated by gunslingers of truly exceptional courage. These gunslingers had by this time shown considerable performance consistency. Therefore, the authors stated, it was time for this attractive mother lode to be discovered by 'responsible' investors."

Louis Alpinieri

"Life insurance is a value-added portfolio asset, an eye-opening concept that can bring real benefits to all readers looking to diversify their opportunities and risks."

Richard Feinberg, Business Consultant and Ph.D. in International Economics, Stanford University

"David clearly has an in-depth understanding of the insurance market as well as investments and what it takes to make and preserve money. His approach is different from what one typically hears, but it is a must to follow because the entire presentation is based on common sense and logic. After reading the book, it is easy to understand why he is a leader in the industry."

Lee Johnson, Ph.D., CEO, Casa Palmera Care Center

"David has become a trusted friend of ours since we met to evaluate our life insurance needs. Considering life insurance an asset instead of an expense was a new thought process for us. We highly recommend his book as a valuable tool to start thinking of investment-grade life insurance as a way to protect yourself and your family for generations to come."

Richard & Stephanie Mirer, Founders, Mirror Wine Company, Napa Valley

"David's book has guided us on the 'best' path possible to acquiring real assets totally uncorrelated to the stock and real estate markets. The difference between a pretax equivalent IRR that we have to earn versus the tax-free IRR of life insurance is sobering! We finally grasp and understand the certainty that life insurance delivers."

Mark & Dina Call, Authors of *The Book on WebCasting*

"David's rich experience in business is reflected in his insights about how sophisticated clients purchase life insurance. I have heard David present often to other life insurance professionals and take them to a higher understanding of the products they help clients purchase. This book will certainly elevate the consumer's and the agent's understanding of this incredible financial product known as life insurance."

Bob Carter, President, Lion Street, Inc.

"Can a book make you wealthy? This one can. Buy it. Study it. Live it."

John & Jan Greene, Founders, PhoneBurner.com

"What a well-written piece. Not only educational, but also interesting. The style of writing takes a subject of pragmatic relevance and spins it in an interesting and heartfelt tale that captivates the reader's attention. Well done and incredibly interesting."

Jeff & Tricia Edwards

"A powerful guide about tax-free money that captivates, teaches, and stimulates new ideas."

Simon Grabowski, CEO, Implix

"If books could be mandated, *The Secret Asset* should be mandatory reading. Finally, our family understands the enormous value proposition in owning as much life insurance as we can buy."

Scott & Erika Laing

"David is brilliant in explaining how life insurance is one of the most valuable assets in a financial plan. He certainly understands the mathematics and explains it in a simple manner. This is great reading!"

Bill Pollakov, CEO, The Pollakov Group

"Thank God *The Secret Asset* is a secret no more! I was fortunate enough to make it to the National Football League; unfortunately, I was clear I was never the smartest guy in the room (even when I was the only one in it!). The many years of smashing my head against the wall a hundred times a day in the NFL sure didn't help my situation either! Thanks to David, I can now finally understand what others have been trying to explain to me for years about investment-grade life insurance. Thanks, David, for bringing it down to my level!"

Sean McNanie, National Football League Player (1984–1991)

Books and Programs
by David D'Arcangelo

Wealth Talk (1993)

Money Smart (1994)

Strike It Rich (1995)

Wealth Starts at Home (1997)

Cash Flow Marketing (1998)

The Secret Asset (2011)

THE SECRET
ASSET

THE SECRET
ASSET

Making Millions with
Investment-Grade Life Insurance

How our family made over $100 million buying investment-grade life insurance, and what you need to know about the greatest asset you don't already own, don't own enough of, or own incorrectly.

☙

DAVID D'ARCANGELO

Redlands Press

Published by Redlands Press.

8910 University Center Lane, Suite 425
San Diego, CA 92122
858-638-1750
www.TheSecretAsset.com

To order additional copies: www.TheSecretAsset.com

Cover and interior design: Erica Jennings, www.jenningsdesignonline.com

Cover photo: Getty/PhotoAlto Agency

ISBN-13: 978-0-615-44302-7

LCCN: 2011921371

Printed in the United States of America.

10 9 8 7 6 5 4 3 2 1

To my wife, Carrie;

my daughter, Ava Bella;

my great friend from college, Randy Perkins;

and my wonderful 12/10/2010 Hoffman Institute process family and friends Shannon, Marc, Brian, Mel, Beth, Joey, Nancy, Cari, Bruce, Gloria, Aideen, Maggie, Michael, Laila, Rachel, Ciuin, Laura Anne, Karen, Christy, Robin, Andrea, Petra, Thomas, Beth, Cherie, Heidi, Jay, Sean, and last but not least, teachers Mary, Sharon, Laurel, and Big Ed.

|CONTENTS

| PREFACE

This book would not have been possible if my college room-mate and business partner, Randy Perkins, had not called me in 2006 and invited me to join him in what I call the "investment-grade life insurance" business.

I'm not sure words can properly describe or even remotely do justice to the titanic life force of positivity that is Randy Perkins, so I'll just say this: Randy is the guy most guys want to be but never have the guts (or the smarts) to become. He's the life of the party and the smartest guy in the room (although he'd never admit it to it).

I met Randy when we were freshmen at the University of Redlands. We both played sports. Randy was a bruising college basketball power forward who could actually shoot and handle the ball, while I was a deceptively quick college football player who used hustle and heart to make up for what I lacked in size. Even though we excelled in our respective sports, we had no delusions about our pro prospects. I knew the NFL would never consider a 5'8", 185-pound running back with a 4.6 forty. Randy knew the NBA wasn't looking for a 6'4" forward with a bad knee. Knowing our futures weren't in sports liberated us in many ways.

We couldn't get enough out of the experience college offered, attacking the books with gusto and enjoying an all-star social life. I had made a friend for life in Randy Perkins.

After college, Randy went on to unparalleled success, and in 1983, I joined him in the financial business. We had a blast! We were as success-ful as we ever dreamed. Eventually, Randy retired (I don't even think he was forty!) to coach his children's sports teams, and I sold my day-to-day business to a division of a New York Stock Exchange company in 2003. I went on to build a number of businesses, write books and training programs, host a TV show, and ultimately, become the founder and chairman of one American Stock Exchange company and the president of another.

For the past several years, I've used the knowledge I gained from working with Randy—and the success I've had making the family in this book more than $100 million—to help people make more money with less risk. I realized that I could reach more people by putting all this knowledge into a book so people like you could fully understand why investment-grade life insurance is one of the greatest assets you have for building family wealth.

While "bad information leads to bad decisions," the opposite can just as easily be true. So here's truly "good information" on investment-grade life insurance. I've written this book using a fictional family, which closely resembles my own, to illustrate the various strategies and techniques involved in this genuine "revolution." It's my sincere hope that you not only enjoy the book, but also learn and apply it to your life and family—that you may make "good decisions" buying investment-grade life insurance.

| INTRODUCTION

The following story revolves around a fictitious family, but the strategies contained within are anything but fictitious. They're real. They are the same ones I help really smart, wealthy people own. Investment-grade life insurance can create unfathomable wealth, not only during your lifetime, but also for generations to come.

ABOUT THE FAMILY

To demonstrate how these investment-grade life insurance policies can be used, I've created a typical all-American, middle-class family covering four generations—grandparents, parents, children, and grandchildren.

The book is written in the first person and narrated by one of the children who happens to be a financial strategist—me. I demonstrate how investment-grade life insurance made the family over $100 million dollars—a return so big you'd think it was the gross national product of a small third-world republic. Yes, a nine-figure return!

The story starts with a fairly simple moneymaking adventure with the grandparents, shifts to the parents, and finally ends with my brother and his children. This smart, successful family wanted to create a family legacy with a lot more cash at every level of the family tree. They figured out a strategy that allowed them to make money coming and going. They did the math and realized they could get a safer, better rate of return on their money by buying investment-grade life insurance on every member of the family.

The only piece that is left out of the story is what your money tree could look like when you replace my family with your own. Just imagine!

ABOUT THE STRATEGIES

This is, ultimately, a story about creating wealth by betting on you. And why not bet on you? After all, no one else is going to make you wealthy.

So, as you read along, simply substitute your own family and relationships into each strategy. Then, project how much wealth you can accumulate. I use larger examples in the book for impact; however, these strategies can work for you if you qualify.

You will see examples of life insurance strategies on one life and some on two lives, what we call "second-to-die" policies that are typically for a husband and wife. Keep in mind that there is flexibility that will allow you to benefit from buying a second-to-die policy on you and an ex-spouse or any two family members. If you are buying a policy and you or the second person is uninsurable, one strategy is to borrow a life or, in other words, use a surrogate insured.

It's that simple.

Every strategy that's outlined in the book is scalable. For instance, if the net worth of your family is $100,000 or $1 billion, just scale my examples up or down accordingly. That way, you can personalize this astounding opportunity for your own particular needs.

I will tell you that there are hundreds of variations to the strategies I use in the book—too many to include in this story. While the ones I have used have been created for impact, other variations may offer even better opportunities. The idea is to open your mind to these new possibilities and then seek help from a really smart, licensed, qualified life insurance agent.

It's my sincere hope that this story—these strategies and truly astounding figures—permanently changes your thinking about how you and your family can create and perpetuate previously unimaginable amounts of wealth during your lifetime. You can dramatically increase the size of your family's legacy by millions—if not tens of millions or even hundreds of millions—of dollars.

ABOUT INVESTMENT-GRADE LIFE INSURANCE

Quick question: Do you own life insurance or do you own investment-grade life insurance?

The main takeaway I want you to have from reading this book is the term *investment-grade life insurance.* Through the examples used in the story, you will come to understand the true meaning of this term and how it can change your life—and the lives of your family members for generations to come.

Investment-grade is what I use to describe a life insurance policy that has been designed by the life insurance agent to optimize the performance of the policy. It can be the most consumer-friendly, opportunistic financial vehicle when it's designed and purchased correctly. The results can be so compelling that you will be forced to ask yourself, "What percent of investment-grade life insurance do I want my family to own in our portfolio?"

Life insurance is a portfolio asset, just like stocks, bonds, and real estate. It can be bought at a net-zero cost, minimum-funded, over-funded, gifted, financed, 1035 exchanged, collateralized, generation skipped, and held until death, when the heirs can collect the insurance benefit without sky-high income and estate taxes.

ABOUT THE POLICY EXAMPLES

The examples of policies used in the book, such as those on the lives of Grandpa John, Grandpa Fred, and others, are single-life policies and pay the stated death benefit upon the death of the insured. In some cases, I have used policies on two lives, the second-to-die policies I previously mentioned, because they pay off at the second death.

Many of the policy examples are "current assumption" examples, and some are "guaranteed" examples of policies. The point to remember is that current assumption policies are based on current assumptions of interest rates, mortality charges, and expenses. Guaranteed policies contractually guarantee your policy for the period of time you choose at purchase. Current assumption policies are generally less expensive than guaranteed policies.

Also, I use some policies designed to go to age 100 to prudently save premium cost, even though companies now produce polices that go to age 121. The policy numerical illustrations are designed to help demonstrate the concept presented and represent no specific policy or company. These examples are not designed to be life insurance illustrations. Complete illustrations can be designed and obtained from your life insurance professional based on your own personal information and objectives. Actual life insurance policy illustrations and policy results will vary based on a number of factors such as policy type, design, health rating, and performance.

Since this is a fictional story about a family, I have taken liberties to dramatize opportunities and possibilities. The characters, places, and names in this book, with the exception of my family, are fictional and are in no way intended to depict anyone in real life. Keep in mind that the illustration examples in this book are just that: examples. The information provided is general and should not be considered legal or tax advice. Consult with a legal or tax professional regarding your unique tax situations.

PART 1

BUILD A FAMILY LEGACY

CHAPTER 1
MEET THE FAMILY

So let me introduce you to my family.

BIG MIKE

Big Mike is just that—big. He has hands the size of a prizefighter and legs that double as tree-trunks. Physically, he is the classic, almost stereotypical Italian you might see in *The Godfather*; however, though he has a dominant personality to go with the looks, he is so mild mannered and kind hearted that he'd never last a day with the Corleones. My dad also has a financial mind that could compete with the whiz kids on Wall Street.

MOM

My saintly mother gave birth to four boys within a five-year span. I still have no idea how she managed to do it. There were so many fights at our house that I've often wondered what was worse for her—giving birth four times in five years or raising us during the next seventeen years. She'd never answer this, of course—too much class—but it is almost shocking we didn't end up as professional boxers or wrestlers.

GRANDPA JOHN

My dad's father, who had grown up poor in Italy, came to the United States in 1920. He had arrived at Ellis Island with Grandma and $13 in his pocket. Grandpa John was a hard-working man who worked diligently to become financially successful. He eventually turned his popular auto lubrication shop into a successful fifty-five unit franchise. A devoted family man, his one wish was to leave an enduring legacy for future generations.

GRANDMA

Grandma was the love of Grandpa John's life. His soul mate. She was a strong woman with a classic dry wit. She loved flowers and turn-of-the-century furniture. She absolutely detested Grandpa John's posse of three hunting beagles that managed to take over the back yard and, quite frequently, dig up all her prized flower beds.

GRANDPA FRED

My mother's father was definitely an independent thinker, a trait he passed along to his four grandsons. He had the most wonderful, colorful stories and a strong opinion about herd mentality. Grandpa Fred would always park as close as he could to a store entrance—"because just as many people leave from the front as the back"—and he felt the need to point out that two-lane freeway exit ramps always had more cars in the farthest right-turn lane and only two or three in the second right-turn lane, which just completely baffled him and led him to conclude that "the masses are almost never right."

TERRY

Our other grandmother was Grandpa Fred's wife, whom we always called Terry. She was by far the best cook, most eloquent speaker, and classiest dresser of anyone in our family (or surrounding neighborhoods, for that matter). Some people just carry themselves so well that they command respect—and that was Terry. She was a college graduate who served as Grandpa Fred's financial bookkeeper for his business and residence. Terry was the "what if things don't go as planned" conscience guiding Grandpa Fred's most important decisions.

MICHAEL

My brother Michael is the oldest of Big Mike and Mom's four children. The technology brain of the family, he is quiet, serious, focused, and an absolute whiz with computers. His propensity for numbers—inherited from Big Mike, no doubt—and seemingly endless stockpile of cash made him the perfect banker when we were kids. He had no problem lending us money (for a small profit). If you paid him back on time, you were given the privilege of borrowing more. If you didn't, he would give you three things: an extension, a penalty payment, and a whup-pin' that would take the better part of the day to recover from. A born leader, Michael is a commander in the Navy Reserve SeaBee Division, and is married with two boys, William and Robert.

JOHN

Long, lanky, and balding. That's my brother John, the third child. John is definitely the most creative person in our family. We didn't have a lot of toys as kids, but what we lacked in merchandise, Johnny made up for with his imagination. He was also the announcer and pitcher when we played waffle ball, the referee/player when we played basketball in our backyard, and the dealer when we played cards. Johnny graduated from college and eventually went to work as a tester on the space shuttle in Southern California. He married, moved to Florida where he worked at Cape Canaveral, and then moved to his wife Mary's hometown in western Pennsylvania. Johnny and Mary have four children—Katy, Theresa, John Jr., and Christopher.

TOMMY

My youngest brother, Tommy, is an incredibly intelligent, perceptive, and honest man. He has the type of personality that draws you in and immediately puts you at ease. A successful broker at a large financial institution, Tommy is also a tremendous golfer, hunter, fisherman, and—most importantly—husband and father. He is married to Barbara and has four children—Gena, John, Jack, and Ellen. I bet I have talked to Tommy at least once a day since 1978.

DAVID

That's me. I am the second oldest of the four wild, wonderfully rambunctious brothers. It's been said that the second child constantly tries hard to keep up with his or her older sibling, who typically gets all the attention, and that was definitely me. So far, I've been able to keep up with Michael in one area: I have two beautiful children as well, Ava and Bella.

So that's my family. We're close (even though we're spread around the country), we're loving, and we're happy. Oh, and we're also all millionaires thanks to discipline and something called investment-grade-designed life insurance.

THE DINNER TABLE

Like most large Italian-American families, we had a weekly family dinner every Sunday at 6:00 P.M. sharp, right after all our friends and relatives who had come over for the weekly Sunday-afternoon gathering left.

Looking back, I now understand that it wasn't just a family tradition that brought everyone over to my house once a week. You see, my dad—Big Mike—had achieved so much financial success that he had earned the respect of everyone in my family and the community as well. My childhood home was the family gathering place for as far back as I can remember.

Big Mike loved numbers because numbers were logical and made sense—at least to him. His mind was razor sharp, and he had an uncanny eye for detail. This basically meant he was forever studying the math behind every financial decision. One of Big Mike's favorite sayings was, "If too many pieces have to align for the deal to work, the odds are it will never happen."

I learned so many valuable things from Big Mike, but it's his "Business Commandments" that remain with me to this day. It could be because he'd repeat them over and over to us kids, just like our Sunday school teachers made us repeat the Ten Commandments. Big Mike would be working in the yard, cutting firewood or the grass, and he would just stop and lay one of those commandments on us.

It did not matter how many of us kids were around, as long as there was someone to listen. One day I was helping him out around the house, and he said, "The person who understands the math always controls the deal." I nodded my head as if I knew what he was talking about, but it wasn't until many years later that I truly understood where he was coming from.

Big Mike's knack for understanding math rubbed off on his sons, because the four of us all learned how to decipher and critique the major-league box scores of the Boston Red Sox, Celtics, Bruins, and New England Patriots before we mastered the multiplication tables.

However, it was his militant attention to detail and connect-the-dots thought process that drove my brothers and me crazy well into our adult years. We were prepared every Sunday night to hear his latest rant.

And so it was this one Sunday night that the four of us gathered around the dinner table and braced ourselves for more of the same. However, on this night, Big Mike looked devastated. He hadn't touched his favorite dinner—medium-rare cowboy steak with sweet potatoes, brown gravy, and broccoli. And my three brothers and I were just about to understand why.

Before Big Mike said something important, he always cleared his throat. And that's just what he did. A low, gravelly "ah-hem" rumbled out and then, in a voice that wavered ever so slightly, he told us that his dad, our grandfather, had suffered a massive heart attack while driving home that morning. Grandpa John was gone.

I had never known anyone who had died until my grandfather passed away that day. Big Mike did his best to describe the accident. He told us that Grandpa John had been only two blocks from his house when the crash had occurred, and that at least three other people were taken to the hospital.

Grandpa John had always been vibrant and healthy. He had loved to boast that he was "seventy-nine years young," and that "you only get old when you start acting old." And now Grandpa John was dead. All I remember is feeling empty and confused, as if someone punched me in the gut. Death had never been so close to me before. It had always stayed far enough away that I considered it no different than being reported absent from school or being on a long summer vacation.

Obviously, what I failed to grasp was death's permanence. Vacations ended; death didn't. I realized this when Big Mike finally stopped being stoic and let the realization of his father's death wash over him. Tears welled up in his eyes (that he fought like hell to hold back), and eventually the enormity of the loss overcame him and he collapsed into his favorite chair, covering his grief-stricken face with those enormous, immaculately manicured hands of his. And then he mumbled, "Poor Grandma."

Grandma was Grandpa John's wife of fifty plus years and the love of his life. How was she going to live without her soul mate? I had no idea, but I knew that years earlier we'd prepared for this awful moment properly and with sober conviction and clear heads. We'd helped our family prepare a transition plan based around each generation's leaving an enduring and positive family and community financial legacy.

When I first started helping people acquire life insurance, I quickly distinguished myself by applying the same tenacious work ethic my own family had modeled so well for me. But it wasn't until I had truly achieved acute mathematical understanding of life insurance policy design that Big Mike finally approved purchasing a $4 million life insurance policy on Grandpa John. This was ten years ago, when Grandpa John was sixty-nine.

The idea was simple. Purchase an investment-grade life insurance policy with the option to *profit* at different phases of his life, with Grandma collecting the death benefit if he died unexpectedly. An investment-grade policy, I had told Big Mike, opened the vault on the life insurance contract, delivering significant financial options to the consumer he or she may have never thought possible.

Luckily, Big Mike had used his gift for facts and figures and realized that the family would collect the $4 million tax-free death benefit. He didn't believe the return on the premiums paid would be almost 400 percent at life expectancy—but then we all had wished Grandpa John would live a long life. However, now with his passing, his legacy would begin anew, and his life would resonate for generations to come with the addition of the $4 million income- and estate-tax-free dollars.

When I had first presented this strategy to Big Mike, his response was exactly the same as almost everyone else I've ever talked to about it: "No, I don't need life insurance."

Look, I get it. Many people don't like or buy life insurance, and generally the ones who do don't buy enough, are underinsured, or worse, don't take the financial rewards seriously enough. And I know that talking about life insurance can be creepy. But this is what I say to people when they say they don't want to buy life insurance: "I know you don't, but . . . do you like making money?"

I'm always careful to give my response as genuinely as I possibly can, without an ounce of irony or too-clever sarcasm. My sincerity is authentic—mainly because I'm a lousy actor and I've learned the hard way that I can't sell something I don't believe in. Nor can I manipulate good, well-meaning people into taking a financial step they don't understand or just aren't emotionally ready to grasp.

But the truth is that what those people ultimately learn is this: "Live or die, you can win!"

LIVE OR DIE, YOU WIN

A lot has changed in the life insurance business since I sold my original business in 1993 and came back into it. *And, quite frankly, these changes are so radical and could have a profound effect on every American family, regardless of their worth, that I'm shocked so few people even know about it, much less understand it.* Hopefully, one day everyone will.

However, my only concern right now is that anyone taking the time and making the effort to read this book understands this unparalleled opportunity.

The wealthy are always ahead of the curve when it comes to using various financial tools and services. How do you think old money got that way? And today, the wealthy are buying investment-grade life insurance just like they would any other prized asset. It's no different to them than buying real estate or stocks and bonds on the cheap.

If you like to make a lot of money—and if you like your family to make well-informed business decisions—you need access to new information so you can make a new decision.

And those decisions begin to change when you *stop thinking of life insurance as an expense* and *start thinking of life insurance as a portfolio asset!* Again, similar to real estate or stocks, you can now buy it, hold it, gift it, generation skip it, 1035 exchange it, or even turn it into a tax-free supplemental retirement plan—all while you're still alive. Wow!

Think of buying life insurance as investing in yourself. Hasn't that always been your best investment?

But to see it that way, you truly have to shift your thinking. Buying life insurance isn't an expense; it's not another monthly bill. It's a portfolio asset.

Do you complain about the "expense" of having your money managed in mutual funds or paying accountants and money managers?

Do you complain about the "expense" of buying or investing in real estate? Well, you might! But I hope you see my point here.

This powerful asset deserves—no, it *demands*—a place in your financial pantheon. Your portfolio, regardless of the size of your investments, should be as diversified as possible. Most portfolios have real estate, stocks, bonds, and cash, but where is the investment-grade life insurance? Nowhere or not enough.

Those in the know are repositioning their portfolios with the addition of investment-grade life insurance because, unlike real estate, stocks, bonds, and cash, it is not market correlated and has serious returns and tax benefits!

Big Mike would never have even considered buying life insurance for Grandpa John unless it could have competed and even beat their safe to moderate-risk investments. Otherwise, why buy life insurance if you could get a better tax-free return buying conservative stocks, bonds, or other investments?

Not only can life insurance compete or even beat those safe to moderate-risk investments, there's substantially less risk! How do I know this? Because, like Big Mike, I inherited a love for math. I also knew that there was no way Big Mike would buy anything without seriously crunching the numbers and that Grandpa John had a real disdain for the whole concept of life insurance.

So I worked out a formula that proved how tax-free life insurance benefits beat safe to moderate-risk investments in their portfolios, both during and after Grandpa John's lifetime.

In other words, I showed them how to make money with life insurance while they were alive, and how their beneficiaries collect an even higher death benefit after they died.

If you're keeping score at home, that's Win, Win, Win.

Win for everyone involved.

Know any other investments like that?

Now even though the following is a little, um, tacky (I prefer colorful), I still find it effective, even if it does cross the line on sensibility or just good manners.

If we are all going to die someday, why do it for FREE?

I mean, really, why?

As far as I'm concerned, it's incredibly tacky *not to* ask this question.

So let's ask it.

Could Grandpa John have received a better return on his money buying a life insurance policy on himself than he did on investing "safely" in United States Treasuries paying 1–3 percent, corporate bonds around 5 percent, and even his portfolio of stocks, which declined more than 50 percent in the last downturn?

Grandpa John had proudly bragged to me that his stocks were coming back. In fact, they had bounced back 50 percent. I didn't have the heart to tell Grandpa John that he'd still be down $250,000, or 25 percent, even with that impressive bounce-back. You see, he needed to return 100 percent just to break even on losing 50 percent.

Confusing? Well let's break it down to simple numbers.

$1 million minus 50% = $500,000

$500,000 plus 50% = $750,000

Summary: a loss of $250,000 from the starting point of $1 million.

LIFE INSURANCE: THE NEW ASSET CLASS

The proposal I made was simple: buy three policies.

1. A policy on Grandpa John's life,
2. A policy on Grandma's life (I'll share in the next chapter), and
3. A combined policy on Grandpa John and Grandma's lives.

First things first, let's talk about #1, the policy on Grandpa John.

"What's the best investment you've ever made?" I asked Grandpa John one day when I was just beginning my career. Without hesitating, he responded that betting/investing on/in himself was by far his best bet. His logic was simple: that's how he had made the most money.

I'll never forget what Grandpa John whispered in my ear after one of our late-night business sessions with Big Mike: "No one cares about you and your money more than you do. When I opened my first garage, no one believed in me or my vision, no one invested a single dime other than me, and no bank would bail me out if I didn't succeed."

"Do you think that's why you made it—because you didn't have any other alternative?" I asked.

"Oh, I had choices. We all have them. I could've managed someone else's shop or, who knows, I might've ended up selling cars instead of fixing them. The point is, I didn't much care for working for other people and making them all sorts of money while I lived paycheck to paycheck. So I made up my mind to do whatever it took to become an owner, not just an employee. I bet on myself, and I became my own man, the architect of my destiny."

I couldn't have said it better. Thanks to Grandpa John's timeless advice and priceless life lesson, I knew what I had to do. I didn't know exactly how I was going to do it, but the one thing I did know was that it was time. Time to let the mainstream know that life insurance was now designed just like any other asset. Why should only the wealthy and elite enjoy the amazing benefits of investment-grade life insurance?

Somehow, I had to transform an old way of thinking into a new way of thinking—and then I had to change people's behavior. There was only one way either of those things was going to be possible: make people a lot of money!

And so I began crafting a formula for a new business model that sought to transform not only perception but behavior as well. I had to prove that this life insurance strategy was one of the safest propositions one could find.

When I presented this strategy to Grandpa John, his eyes widened and he said, "David, why would I buy life insurance? Life's been good to me. I've been blessed and worked hard and succeeded beyond my wildest dreams. Successful people don't buy life insurance." He paused. "Do they?"

I had seen Grandpa John's inquisitive look on many other faces, and I knew exactly what I had to do to get the lightbulb to go on inside his head. One of the most important things I tell young people starting out in sales, regardless of what they're selling, is that "a confused mind says no."

I needed to turn Grandpa John's confusion into crystal-clear clarity. First, that meant reframing the very concept of life insurance itself. I had to get him to see it as an asset in his portfolio and not as another monthly bill.

I looked directly at Grandpa John and said, "Grandpa John, do you mind if I ask you a few questions?"

"Fire away!" he answered.

"How much life insurance would you buy if life insurance had no cost?"

"Um, I guess I'd get as much as they would sell me."

"Okay, great. So Grandpa John, how much life insurance do you currently own?"

"I have a $1 million policy I bought years and years ago."

"Why do you only own a $1 million policy when you just told me you would buy the maximum they would sell you?"

"Because I have to pay for it," he said, chuckling.

"So, Grandpa John, if I understand you correctly, you really like life insurance, you just don't like paying for it, correct?"

"Ah, I never thought of it that way, but I guess you're right."

"Grandpa John, if I could show you how to buy life insurance at a net-zero cost or even profit from it, how much would you buy?"

"Like I said, I'd buy as much as they would sell me."

CHAPTER 2

WHY SMART PEOPLE MAKE MORE MONEY

Score a victory for me. I had succeeded in helping Grandpa John make the huge shift in his perception, and subsequently his behavior, regarding life insurance.

And score a victory for Grandpa John, too. He had helped me understand why people weren't already locked into great investment-grade life insurance policies. He had confessed that he actually liked life insurance, but wasn't fond of paying for it. Then again, that was probably how Grandpa John felt about paying taxes, too, but I wasn't about to call him on it, especially after we had just replaced a long-standing negative behavior anchor with a positive anchor.

After Big Mike and Grandpa John vetted my portfolio asset strategy with their usual intensity—triple-checking every fact and financial projection—I moved forward with my business proposition. I painstakingly designed a plan to build our family legacy—now and for future generations.

I knew the goals had to be precise and clearly defined, so I narrowed them down to three key steps and then described the result we hoped to achieve:

1. Purchase $4 million of life insurance on Grandpa John's life as soon as possible.

2. Calculate the internal rate of return (IRR) the death benefit would provide on an annual basis, based on the total premiums paid.

3. Structure the policy with minimum out-of-pocket costs and the highest potential return based on Grandpa John's financial objectives.

KNOW THE ANSWERS BEFORE THE TEST

The Social Security Administration publishes average life-expectancy tables for both males and females. It just makes sense to know your average life expectancy so you can review the ultimate return possibilities on the premiums you will pay.

Since planning would be much easier if we knew Grandpa John's average life expectancy, we reviewed the life expectancy tables for people of his current age, sixty-nine. (Just remember that general life expectancy tables don't tell you when you die; they just provide you with the average for people in your same category.)

There was nothing gloomy about reviewing these tables. In fact, it was extremely helpful to us to know what Grandpa John's average life expectancy was for his age group. We got a better understanding of the mathematics of life insurance, which enabled me to structure the premiums to be the smallest amount possible prior to hitting that life expectancy.

Less cash in means more cash out.

This means that if Grandpa John had an average life expectancy of eighty-three versus ninety-three, then we could structure the premiums to potentially save him a lot of money. How? Well, many life insurance companies allow you to run the standard insurance illustrations to age 120. If Grandpa had a median life expectancy of eighty-three, then we could potentially save many premium dollars by running the illustration to age ninety-five or one hundred, twelve to seventeen years past his average life expectancy. Why run illustrations to 120 if the life expectancy is age eighty-three? Paying lower annual premiums saves big money. I could argue this point both ways, but just stay with me to open up our possibility thinking.

The chart below displays the average life expectancy for men and women. Grandpa John was sixty-nine years old when we first started planning his policy. By using this chart, we learned that the average male his age had a life expectancy of 14.22 more years. Therefore, on average, men Grandpa John's age live to be 83.22.

Planning is helpful when you know the averages in advance.

Social Security Administration Period Life Tables 2006[1]		
	Male	**Female**
Exact Age	**Life Expectancy (yrs)**	**Life Expectancy (yrs)**
10	65.80	70.82
20	56.13	60.99
30	46.89	51.28
40	37.61	41.70
45	33.11	37.04
50	28.78	32.49
55	24.66	28.07
60	20.70	23.78
65	16.17	19.72
69	**14.22**	**16.64**
70	13.55	15.90
75	10.46	12.43
80	7.78	9.33
85	5.56	6.68
90	3.84	4.62
95	2.67	3.20
100	2.01	2.35

1 The population comprised of (i) residents of the 50 states and the District of Columbia (adjusted for net census undercount); (ii) civilian residents of Puerto Rico, the Virgin Islands, Guam, American Samoa, and the Northern Mariana Islands; (iii) federal civilian employees and persons in the US Armed Forces abroad and their dependents; (iv) crew members of merchant vessels; and (v) all other US citizens abroad.

Source: http://www.ssa.gov/OACT/STATS/table4c6.html

Now that we knew Grandpa John's median life expectancy was 83.22 (age 69 + 14.22 years = 83.22), I could customize a policy with equal annual premiums every year for life until age 120 (or any age prior, such as 100). In many cases, this will reduce the premiums. (I will keep the design simple on this policy and expand out flexibility and opportunities, thinking outside the box, so to speak, as we move to other examples in later chapters.)

I designed a simple $4 million life insurance policy on Grandpa John to get us started, which at his age and health rating, required an annual premium of $94,839.

Let's round that off to $100,000 to illustrate a point for a moment. Grandpa John bought the policy at age sixty-nine, and the life insurance death benefit was $4 million. The worst-case scenario financially was that he would pay premiums for forty years totaling $4 million, and die at the age of 109. In that case, he would have broken even because he paid in a total of $4 million and there was a $4 million benefit.

Let's start with the big picture. What were the chances of Grandpa John's living to age 109? About as good a chance as me costarring with Brad Pitt in a remake of *Gone with the Wind*. Zero. Zilch. Nada.

REVERSE DOLLAR COST AVERAGE

Remember, we already knew Grandpa John's average life expectancy when he purchased his policy was 14.22 years (age 83.22) and not forty years (age 109).

My recommendation was to dollar cost average $94,839 annually out of his investment portfolio that was earning 1 percent in short-term treasuries, 5 percent in bonds, and -20 percent to +20 percent in the stock market into a life insurance contract to control a potential $4 million life insurance benefit. The performance of this policy is correlated to his life expectancy and not the stock, bond, or real estate market.

That meant that for the entire decade of his seventies, Grandpa John could monitor taxes, the economy, family changes, and his health while diversifying his investment portfolio $94,839 per year on a product that pays a tax-free $4 million to his wife upon his death.

Since the prior ten years had produced a flat or negative rate of return on many invested portfolios, Grandpa John had been intelligently diversifying by dollar cost averaging out of a negative return portfolio and into a tax-free $4 million windfall.

If your personal or family net worth and cash flow are lower or higher, just buy 75 percent, 50 percent, or 25 percent less or more than the examples I have illustrated. The numbers adjust on a pro-rata basis up or down for the same ages and health, and the returns are exactly the same.

Let's look at the actual numbers for this strategy. If my example is a $4 million policy, a $2 million policy would cut the premiums by 50 percent; a $1 million policy would reduce the premiums by 50 percent from the $2 million policy for the same age and health. Conversely, it's the exact same math if you go 25 percent, 50 percent, or 100 percent higher.

Let's look at the general mathematical design of Grandpa John's policy.

IRR Annually Based on Policy Structure – Age at End of Year					
Age	Premiums	Premiums as a % of Death Benefit (DB)	Death Benefit	Internal Rate of Return (IRR) on DB*	Tax Equivalent IRR (NDB)**
70	$94,839	2.37%	$4,000,000	4,117.66%	6334.86%
71	$94,839	2.37%	$4,000,000	501.36%	771.32%
72	$94,839	2.37%	$4,000,000	209.10%	321.69%
73	$94,839	2.37%	$4,000,000	121.68%	187.21%
74	$94,839	2.37%	$4,000,000	83.08%	126.28%
75	$94,839	2.37%	$4,000,000	60.08%	92.44%
76	$94,839	2.37%	$4,000,000	46.30%	71.24%
77	$94,839	2.37%	$4,000,000	36.96%	56.86%
78	$94,839	2.37%	$4,000,000	30.26%	48.56%
79	$94,839	2.37%	$4,000,000	25.25%	38.35%
80	$94,839	2.37%	$4,000,000	21.39%	32.90%

IRR Annually Based on Policy Structure – Age at End of Year					
Age	Premiums	Premiums as a % of Death Benefit (DB)	Death Benefit	Internal Rate of Return (IRR) on DB*	Tax Equivalent IRR (NDB)**
81	$94,839	2.37%	$4,000,000	18.32%	28.19%
82	$94,839	2.37%	$4,000,000	15.85%	24.38%
83	$94,839	2.37%	$4,000,000	13.81%	21.25%
Average Life Expectancy 83 years					
84	$94,839	2.37%	$4,000,000	12.11%	18.63%
85	$94,839	2.37%	$4,000,000	10.68%	16.43%
86	$94,839	2.37%	$4,000,000	9.45%	14.54%
87	$94,839	2.37%	$4,000,000	8.39%	12.91%
88	$94,839	2.37%	$4,000,000	7.47%	11.50%
89	$94,839	2.37%	$4,000,000	6.67%	10.26%
90	$94,839	2.37%	$4,000,000	5.96%	9.17%
91	$94,839	2.37%	$4,000,000	5.33%	8.20%
92	$94,839	2.37%	$4,000,000	4.77%	7.34%
93	$94,839	2.37%	$4,000,000	4.27%	6.56%
94	$94,839	2.37%	$4,000,000	3.82%	5.87%
95	$94,839	2.37%	$4,000,000	3.41%	5.24%
96	$94,839	2.37%	$4,000,000	3.04%	4.67%
97	$94,839	2.37%	$4,000,000	2.70%	4.16%
98	$94,839	2.37%	$4,000,000	2.40%	3.68%
99	$94,839	2.37%	$4,000,000	2.11%	3.25%
100	$94,839	2.37%	$4,000,000	1.81%	2.86%

*IRR on death benefit is the level annual interest rate at which the net annual outlays up to that year accumulated at each and every year to generate the net death benefit shown.

**Tax Equivalent IRR (NDB) is the level annual interest rate at which the net annual outlays up to that year must be accumulated at each and every year to generate after-tax amounts equal to the death benefit shown, assuming a level annual federal income tax rate of 35%. If the net annual outlays were invested in alternative investments subject to income taxes, this is the gross rate of return that would need to be earned so that the accumulated amount net of income taxes would equal the amount reported in the net death benefit column. This figure is intended to help illustrate the potential tax advantages of the life insurance policy and does not represent the rate of return of the life insurance policy itself.

If Grandpa John had passed away at age eighty-three, the original life expectancy at the time of purchase, the internal rate of return would have been 13.81 percent tax free. The tax equivalent return you would have to earn to net 13.81 percent is 21.25 percent in the 35 percent tax bracket.

Think about that. What other investment/business do you have compounding year in and year out at 21.25 percent pretax annually? Real estate? No way.

Nothing is good or bad until we have something to compare it to. So let's illustrate my point. If you paid $1 million for your home and it grew at the compounded rate of 21.25 percent for the same thirteen-year period, it would be worth $12,242,291.

How many people do you know make this type of tax-free return? Even if Grandpa John had lived five years past the average life expectancy, to age eighty-eight, the return would have still been an impressive 7.47 percent (or you would have to earn the taxable equivalent, 11.50 percent in the 35 percent tax bracket).

Conversely, if Grandpa John had died prior to the average life expectancy of eighty-three, the return would increase as stated in the illustration above. So, when Grandpa John died at age seventy-nine, the IRR return was a whopping 25.25 percent tax free. The tax-free equivalent yield you would have to earn to net 25.25 percent would be 35.35 percent in the 35 percent federal tax bracket!

How much life insurance do you own in your portfolio?

Here's a question for you: After taxes, fees, and inflation, what is the net bottom-line rate of return you are receiving in your investment portfolio?

The real answer? The average person I have reviewed earns about 3.0 percent net of taxes, inflation, and fees on average. For example: 10 percent gross return less 3 percent in taxes, 2 percent inflation, and 2 percent fees nets you 3 percent.

In Grandpa John's case, the 25.25 percent return is net after taxes and fees because of the way it was purchased and designed. Subtract an average 3 percent inflation rate and the beneficiaries' internal rate of return is 22.25 percent.

Now let's look at the return and review the math.

LIFE INSURANCE RETURNS

Grandpa John's dollar cost averaged $94,839 out from his investment portfolio and into life insurance with a $4 million tax-free benefit.

Grandpa liked his money to work as hard as he did, and this business proposition was no different.

The first payment of $94,839 controlled a potential $4 million asset.

You are your greatest asset. Why wouldn't you invest in yourself, especially at those potential rates of return?

Grandpa passed away in year ten, after making ten payments of $94,839, totaling $948,390. Grandma collected the $4 million death benefit income-tax free.

Where else do you get a 4.2-to-1 tax-free return on your money over ten years, and with low risk?

Nowhere . . . other than life insurance.

CHAPTER 3
HOW PREMIUMS CAN BE SO LOW— "THE RISK POOL"

So, by now you might be wondering how I got into the financial business. Well, it kind of goes like this.

I graduated from college—the first person in our family to do so—and, much to the dismay of Big Mike, I immediately embarked upon a long-held dream of mine to see the world before life's responsibilities pulled me back to reality.

I must admit that my little adventure was both liberating and rewarding. It was the first time in my adult life I had really done something solely for myself, and the first time I truly realized that life wasn't going to be very fulfilling unless I managed to challenge myself. After all, if I wasn't going to do it, who would?

After I ended my nine-nation journey living on the outskirts of an Egyptian village for a time, I came back to the States. Two years had raced by, and I felt like I had not missed a thing. My only rule back then was that life be ethical, moral, and fun. I had gone through about 70 percent of the stock-picking winnings I had made while I was a college student. And that's when I realized that I liked the freedom that came with money. I had always planned on making quite a bit of money, but now I was mentally ready to excel at it.

But first I had to ready myself for Big Mike, who was not exactly happy with me. He sat me down when I returned from my "extended vacation" and talked a lot about the grief his friends were giving him for having a hotshot, globe-trotting, temporarily unemployed college boy for a son.

I apologized to Big Mike—even though I didn't know what I was apologizing for exactly. Actually, I'm not really sure Big Mike was looking for an apology, for he pointed out that those same friends had never taken advantage of all that life had offered them, as I had done.

Of course, the point he was trying to make hit its target. I knew what he was trying to tell me, and since he was fumbling with his words, I let him off the hook.

"Look, Dad, I'm going back to California and getting a job," I announced.

Big Mike was really glad—and relived, I'm sure. He had wanted nothing more in the world than for me to be using my education. He wanted me to succeed, and he pledged to give me his full support.

He did that and more. I ended up in the financial industry and, ultimately, the life insurance business with my force-of-nature college roommate and friend, Randy Perkins.

As I began to succeed, Big Mike began to study up on the life insurance "racket," as he called it. He was hesitant when I suggested the family buy investment-grade life insurance policies. However, after advising Big Mike and Mom through the process from the very beginning, we designed the policies so they worked for our family's unique needs and traditional values.

Big Mike was stunned that the insurance company paid the death benefit on Grandpa John exactly as promised. The truth is I often found myself taking the side of an apologist for big business and corporations when talking to Big Mike. He liked to tease me about it, but I knew how these corporations operated. They worked diligently to maximize their bottom line so they could fulfill their contractual commitments and make decent profits for their shareholders. There was nothing inherently sinister about it. It was just good business.

So when Big Mike was surprised that the life insurance company paid, it was my turn to make fun of him. "That's right, these insurance companies have only been around for the last century by not paying out their policies," I teased.

He still wasn't buying it. He smelled a rat. "I didn't go to a fancy school. The only school I went to was the school of hard knocks, and it gave me a Ph.D. in smelling BS. I paid the premiums on those policies. I did the math myself, and there's no way the company can sustain this kind of return. The numbers just don't work out. How can insurance companies make money this way?"

"They can and they do," I said patiently. "You just need the right figures, Dad. Conceptually, it's just like the insurance you bought to cover Mom's jewelry, trip cancellations, and our car, health, and home. It all works mathematically because of the risk pool. Let me explain it in a simplified manner. The 100 people who insure their jewelry become the same 100 people in the risk pool. If an average of 5 percent had their jewelry stolen, that would translate into a 5-out-of-100 payout ratio from the risk pool. I am grossly simplifying things, but look at it another way: the payments of ninety-five people help support the five people who collect, with enough left over for the insurance company to make a profit. Everyone wins."

He was still skeptical, so I continued on. "In life insurance, there is a benefit provided that helps keep life insurance premiums at some of their lowest rates in thirty years. The life insurance company is obligated to pay out the full policy benefit for their clients who stayed current on their premiums and whose policies remained in force. Like many other types of insurance, you want to guess what percentage of people who buy life insurance policies never stick around to collect the death benefit?"

"Fifty percent?" guessed Big Mike.

"Higher," I replied.

"Sixty-five percent?" Big Mike ventured.

I shook my head. "Higher."

Big Mike grew increasingly frustrated. He guessed 75 percent, and I shook my head again and repeated that the overall percentage of policyholders who do not claim the death benefit is even higher.

"I've been in the wrong business!" he exclaimed. "Can you imagine? Just think about more than three-fourths of a business's customers paying for something and then leaving. It allows the insurance company to use those dollars to subsidize, so to speak, the benefits to the policyholders who go the distance!"

"Yup, that's pretty much what happens," I said.

"Okay. Stop torturing me and tell me already," Big Mike pleaded.

I ended his suffering. "The magic number is up to . . . 88 percent."

I honestly thought Big Mike was going to have a heart attack. Up to eighty-eight out of one hundred? That's means up to seven out of eight people quit!

His eyes opened wide, and I could tell his powerful mind was quickly churning out figures.

"So that's why I don't have to worry about the insurance companies meeting their obligation to Mom and me," he said. "The seven who quit help subsidize the cost of insurance, potentially resulting in lower premiums for the one who stays and goes the distance to collect the large life insurance benefit!"

"Exactly," I replied. "It's not the only reason, but it is another reason why the person who understands the math generally controls the deal. You want to be the one who stays and not the five, six, or seven who quit. That's how you win. Their formulas are pretty much bulletproof. That's why it is so important that anyone who buys should understand the compelling options and the math."

I began to apply my knowledge about how life insurance companies—or the "House"— worked, only I flipped the formulas. It was a pretty radical idea, but I had run some preliminary numbers, and it worked like a charm.

I started by plugging in the numbers and data Big Mike and I had helped generate for the family with investment-grade life insurance. I wanted to create an investment-grade life insurance asset model based on the strategies and lessons I'd picked up helping clients purchase tens of millions of dollars in policies over the years in almost every conceivable situation, as well as those lessons learned in designing the policies for our respective family members.

I'd set out to build a presentation book that I thought might help other families accomplish what Big Mike and I were trying to accomplish for our family. Now I was driven to accomplish something even more ambitious.

CHAPTER 4

IF YOU'RE GOING TO DIE, WHY DO IT FOR FREE?

Grandpa John had always been interested in creating a family legacy. Big Mike thought it came from how poor Grandpa had been growing up and from the long days and longer hours Grandpa had worked in the early years with almost nothing to show for it. On his fifty-fifth birthday, all of Grandpa's lifetime of hard work finally began to pay off.

David Fisher, his attorney, walked into Grandpa John's lube shop and told him that he needed to open another lube shop across the state as quickly as possible. Mr. Fisher shared story after story about the people around town who had moved away, yet still lamented that there wasn't anything close to the quality of service Grandpa John offered. They'd even said they'd pay twice as much as Grandpa John charged just to have Grandpa John down the street.

While getting amazing customer service is rare these days, back when Grandpa John opened his business, it was virtually nonexistent. Yet, Grandpa John based his entire business model on having not just satisfied customers, but ecstatic ones. His motto was, "Always give the customers more value than they believe they're paying for, and you'll create raving fans for life." And that's exactly what he did for twenty years. Clearly, his model worked, as he franchised fifty-five shops in seventeen states.

I reviewed a policy Grandpa John bought on Grandma when we bought his policy. At the time of purchase, Grandma was sixty-eight years old. I took Big Mike and Grandpa John through the same exercise, evaluating Grandma's policy.

Review items:

1. The Social Security Administration Average Life Expectancy Table,
2. Policy premium design for maximum return advantage, and
3. The Internal Rate of Return calculation annually to age 100.

Ten years ago, Big Mike and Grandpa John had called me and asked if I would show them their options for a twenty-year cheap term life insurance policy on Grandma. "Term" insurance specifically applies to a term such as ten, fifteen, or twenty years. Conversely, permanent insurance generally is bought for a lifetime.

Grandma's age group's median life expectancy at the time was 17.4 years.

Social Security Administration Period Life Tables 2006[1]	
Exact Age	Female Life Expectancy (yrs)
10	70.82
20	60.99
30	51.28
40	41.70
45	37.04
50	32.49
55	28.07
60	23.78
65	19.72
68	**17.40**
70	15.90
75	12.43

Social Security Administration Period Life Tables 2006[1]	
Exact Age	**Female Life Expectancy (yrs)**
80	9.33
85	6.68
90	4.62
95	3.20
100	2.35

1 The population comprised of (i) residents of the 50 states and the District of Columbia (adjusted for net census undercount); (ii) civilian residents of Puerto Rico, the Virgin Islands, Guam, American Samoa, and the Northern Mariana Islands; (iii) federal civilian employees and persons in the US Armed Forces abroad and their dependents; (iv) crew members of merchant vessels; and (v) all other US citizens abroad.

Source: http://www.ssa.gov/OACT/STATS/table4c6.html

Basically, that broke down to approximately 50 percent of the people with the same profile dying before 17.4 years and approximately 50 percent dying after 17.4 years. Because we understood these numbers, buying a twenty-year term policy on Grandma was cutting it close, as approximately 50 percent outlive the twenty-year level term policy.

The $4 million term policy's annual premium is $46,510 every year for twenty years. (That's $11,627 per year/million of coverage.)

At the end of five years, the premiums out of pocket total $232,550; after ten years, $465,100; after fifteen years, $697,650; and after twenty years, the premium total is $930,200.

Of course, we all hoped that Grandma would live beyond the twenty years. However, if she had, then the coverage would have been rendered useless, which would have been good for Grandma, but a poor investment since there's no return of the $930,000 in premiums paid.

Grandpa John and Big Mike had been stunned when I had shown them these facts.

"This isn't an acceptable risk because if Grandma's alive after year twenty, which we hope and pray will happen, we're out $930,200! Almost a million bucks gone and no insurance coverage!" said Grandpa John.

$4 Million – Grandma, Preferred Non-Tobacco, Age 68, 20-Year Term Quote		
Year	**Age**	**20-Year Term Annual Premium**
1	68	$46,510
2	69	$46,510
3	70	$46,510
4	71	$46,510
5	72	$46,510
6	73	$46,510
7	74	$46,510
8	75	$46,510
9	76	$46,510
10	77	$46,510
11	78	$46,510
12	79	$46,510
13	80	$46,510
14	81	$46,510
15	82	$46,510
16	83	$46,510
17	84	$46,510
18	85	$46,510
19	86	$46,510
20	87	$46,510
Total Premiums 20 years		**$930,200 Total**
(End Year 20 Policy Is Terminated)		

I understood Grandpa John's logic and went about solving it.

Let's explore the two options for permanent policy design I gave him. First, I designed a $4 million permanent life insurance policy just like the one we had helped Grandpa buy. I used the same annual premium pay model with premiums of $82,442 annually.

That amounted to just 2.06 percent of the death benefit annually. Looked at another way, it would take 48.5 years for the total premiums to equal the $4 million death benefit payoff. Just think about that. Grandma would have needed to live to 117 for them to break even on their $4 million of premiums paid versus the life insurance $4 million benefit payout. Yes, I know there is a time value of money calculation, but I am just making a point.

The odds of Grandma's living to age 117 were zero, considering her life expectancy was only 17.4 more years. Paying premiums of 2.06 percent of the $4 million benefit for 17.4 years is only 35 percent, or $1.4 million, of the $4 million benefit payoff. Grandma could live five years past her original life expectancy at purchase to age ninety and still have a 6.41 percent internal rate or return. In the 35 percent tax bracket, that's a pretax equivalent IRR of approximately 9.86 percent—leaving plenty of room for profit.

Just imagine a 6.41 percent tax-free return net of fees and taxes on a conservative financial vehicle every single year from age sixty-eight to ninety! That is twenty-five years of uninterrupted returns.

Again, let's review the general design mathematics in Grandma's annual-level premium policy.

Grandma – Annual Premium Pay Policy (Age at End of Year)						
Year	Age	Premium	% of Death Benefit	Death Benefit	IRR on Death Benefit	Tax Equivalent IRR on Death Benefit
1	69	$82,442	2.06%	$4,000,000	4751.90%	7,310.61%
2	70	$82,442	2.06%	$4,000,000	548.35%	843.61%
3	71	$82,442	2.06%	$4,000,000	225.96%	347.64%
4	72	$82,442	2.06%	$4,000,000	131.10%	201.70%
5	73	$82,442	2.06%	$4,000,000	88.46%	136.09%
6	74	$82,442	2.06%	$4,000,000	64.88%	99.82%
7	75	$82,442	2.06%	$4,000,000	50.15%	77.15%
8	76	$82,442	2.06%	$4,000,000	40.17%	61.81%
9	77	$82,442	2.06%	$4,000,000	33.03%	50.81%
10	78	$82,442	2.06%	$4,000,000	27.69%	42.60%
11	79	$82,442	2.06%	$4,000,000	23.57%	36.25%

Grandma – Annual Premium Pay Policy (Age at End of Year)						
Year	Age	Premium	% of Death Benefit	Death Benefit	IRR on Death Benefit	Tax Equivalent IRR on Death Benefit
12	80	$82,442	2.06%	$4,000,000	20.30%	31.23%
13	81	$82,442	2.06%	$4,000,000	17.66%	27.17%
14	82	$82,442	2.06%	$4,000,000	15.49%	23.82%
15	83	$82,442	2.06%	$4,000,000	13.67%	21.03%
16	84	$82,442	2.06%	$4,000,000	12.14%	18.67%
17	85	$82,442	2.06%	$4,000,000	10.83%	16.65%
Life Expectancy 17.4 yrs at origination						
18	86	$82,442	2.06%	$4,000,000	9.69%	14.91%
19	87	$82,442	2.06%	$4,000,000	8.71%	13.40%
20	88	$82,442	2.06%	$4,000,000	7.85%	12.07%
21	89	$82,442	2.06%	$4,000,000	7.08%	10.90%
22	90	$82,442	2.06%	$4,000,000	6.41%	9.86%
23	91	$82,442	2.06%	$4,000,000	5.81%	8.93%
24	92	$82,442	2.06%	$4,000,000	5.27%	8.10%
25	93	$82,442	2.06%	$4,000,000	4.78%	7.35%
26	94	$82,442	2.06%	$4,000,000	4.34%	6.68%
27	95	$82,442	2.06%	$4,000,000	3.94%	6.06%
28	96	$82,442	2.06%	$4,000,000	3.58%	5.50%
29	97	$82,442	2.06%	$4,000,000	3.25%	4.99%
30	98	$82,442	2.06%	$4,000,000	2.94%	4.53%
31	99	$82,442	2.06%	$4,000,000	2.66%	4.10%
32	100	$82,442	2.06%	$4,000,000	2.41%	3.70%

As I previously mentioned, Big Mike loved mathematics. He had a real passion for numbers and there were few things he liked more than working numbers until they worked to put him in the best position possible.

He asked me one last question: "Could you please show me one more illustration showing a creative design with a permanent policy? I have a large amount of cash earning almost nothing in US treasuries, and I need a safe place to move it with better returns."

It was a darn good question, and I had wondered why I hadn't thought to show him it already. I showed him the differences between three different styles of insurance.

Option 1.   Twenty-year level term insurance.

Option 2.   Permanent policy design with lifetime annual premiums.

Option 3.   Creative permanent policy design like the one we did for Grandpa John, paying one premium in the first year and then no premiums starting again until Grandma was eighty-one (year thirteen). No premiums in years two, three, four, five, six, seven, eight, nine, ten, eleven, and twelve.

Grandpa John and Big Mike immediately picked Option 3. It was the easiest solution to their problem of finding a more efficient place to warehouse a lump sum of cash. Of course, you could make a case for either Option 1 or Option 2 if the situation were different. It's all personal preference, which is one of the most amazing benefits given to the consumer by most life insurance companies. In this case, the $600,000 savings by year twenty and the eleven years of zero premiums won out.

The bottom line is that the consumer wins with every selection. Even Option 1 can be a winner if the consumer only wants short-term cheap coverage to cover a very definite twenty-year period of risk. Don't like Option 1? That's okay. Like the lower annual premiums of Option 2? Select Option 2. Like the idea of warehousing a lump sum of cash in year one and paying *no* premiums for a while? Select Option 3. Your agent designs, you win! Remember, the person who understands the math controls the deal.

Grandma – Comparison of $4 Million Term, Annual Pay, and Creative Premium Pay Policies Annual Premiums – Age at End of Year						
		(Option 1) Term Insurance	(Option 2) Traditional Design		(Option 3) Creative Design	
Yr	Age	20-Year Term	Perm Policy	IRR	Mike's Design	IRR
1	69	$46,510	$82,442	7,310.61%	$348,000	1,049.43%
2	70	$46,510	$82,442	843.61%	$0	239.03%
3	71	$46,510	$82,442	347.64%	$0	125.68%
4	72	$46,510	$82,442	201.70%	$0	84.13%
5	73	$46,510	$82,442	136.09%	$0	62.97%
6	74	$46,510	$82,442	99.82%	$0	50.23%
7	75	$46,510	$82,442	77.15%	$0	41.74%
8	76	$46,510	$82,442	61.81%	$0	35.69%
9	77	$46,510	$82,442	50.81%	$0	31.17%
10	78	$46,510	$82,442	42.60%	$0	27.66%
11	79	$46,510	$82,442	36.25%	$0	24.86%
12	80	$46,510	$82,442	31.23%	$0	22.57%
13	81	$46,510	$82,442	27.17%	$90,000	20.41%
14	82	$46,510	$82,442	23.82%	$90,000	18.55%
15	83	$46,510	$82,442	21.03%	$90,000	16.92%
16	84	$46,510	$82,442	18.67%	$90,000	15.47%
17	85	$46,510	$82,442	16.65%	$90,000	14.18%
Life Expectancy 17.4 yrs at origination						
18	86	$46,510	$82,442	14.91%	$90,000	13.02%
19	87	$46,510	$82,442	13.40%	$90,000	11.97%
20	88	$46,510	$82,442	12.07%	$90,000	11.02%
Subtotals		$930,200	$1,648,840		$1,068,000	
21	89	Terminated	$82,442	10.90%	$90,000	10.14%
22	90	Terminated	$82,442	9.86%	$90,000	9.34%
23	91	Terminated	$82,442	8.93%	$90,000	8.60%
24	92	Terminated	$82,442	8.10%	$90,000	7.92%
25	93	Terminated	$82,442	7.35%	$90,000	7.29%
26	94	Terminated	$82,442	6.68%	$90,000	6.70%
27	95	Terminated	$82,442	6.06%	$90,000	6.16%

Grandma – Comparison of $4 Million Term, Annual Pay, and Creative Premium Pay Policies Annual Premiums – Age at End of Year						
		(Option 1) Term Insurance	**(Option 2) Traditional Design**		**(Option 3) Creative Design**	
Yr	**Age**	**20-Year Term**	**Perm Policy**	**IRR**	**Mike's Design**	**IRR**
28	96	Terminated	$82,442	5.50%	$90,000	5.66%
29	97	Terminated	$82,442	4.99%	$90,000	5.19%
30	98	Terminated	$82,442	4.53%	$90,000	4.76%
31	99	Terminated	$82,442	4.10%	$90,000	4.36%
32	100	Terminated	$82,442	3.70%	$90,000	3.99%
33	101	Terminated	Terminated		Terminated	

CHAPTER 5

HOW TO MAKE A GOOD DEAL BETTER

Big Mike and Grandpa John had liked every aspect of Option 3. Simple mathematics had shown every possible outcome.

- Warehouse $348,000 in year one on the life insurance policy that was formerly in low-paying investments or cash.

- Pay no premiums in years two, three, four, five, six, seven, eight, nine, ten, eleven, and twelve.

- See what changes during the dozen years between Grandma's age of purchase and her eighty-first birthday . . . health, economy, estate taxes, charitable interests, etc.

- Gift the policy to a favorite charity that Grandpa John and Grandma supported, or to one of their beloved alma maters.

- Transfer the policy to Big Mike and Mom using estate-planning strategies.

Let's say for the sake of this illustration that Grandma aged gracefully as she approached age eighty-one. Instead of losing almost $1 million and having no life insurance based on the term policy, Grandpa John and Big Mike, using Option 3, simply paid the premiums beginning in year thirteen.

Grandpa John and Big Mike were both old and savvy enough to know you don't get anything in this life for free—instead of being exposed to an "unacceptable" risk and losing the whole seven-figure investment if they had purchased term insurance or paid annual premiums in Option 2, they agreed that Option 3 fit their objectives best.

This eliminated the "risk" of losing level term coverage in Option 1—and maximized the benefits made available in Option 3 based on their objectives. Live or die; win–win. Make money buying life insurance.

Either way, we removed the "shot clock" on the life insurance payout of the death benefit. We also removed any anxiety regarding remaining years—the staring down the double barrel of an impossible life decision as the term policy got closer and closer to expiring. Not only would we have forfeited a significant family investment, but we also would have been forced to deal with our elderly and beloved family matriarch's being uninsured.

Big Mike made sure I knew the difference between an "educated'" or "calculated" risk and an "unnecessary" one usually made out of haste and ignorance. He explained to me that the majority of people based the most crucial decisions of their financial lives not on numbers, research, or data, but rather on emotions. That's right. Making decisions this way is no different than playing a hunch at the track or betting on the underdog in the big game because you had a "feeling."

"You can't trust emotions," Big Mike had said. "One day, you might feel one way and the next, you'll feel entirely differently and have no idea why." He had peered into my eyes and asked, "Now, does that sound like a reliable business model to you?"

He shook his head before I could answer. He wasn't discounting the power of being in touch with and understanding your emotions. It was just that he and Grandpa John had seen too many friends and neighbors make quick, emotionally charged decisions that nearly always ended in disaster.

Those poorly thought out decisions had led to dear family friends being forced to sell after ill-advised attempts at opening more stores or expanding. People came to Big Mike and Grandpa John for business advice all the time, but they often didn't agree with or like the assessments and recommendations given to them.

We lost count of how many neighbors had moved out of our middle-class neighborhood and into larger homes in fancier neighborhoods. We had always wished them well and prayed they had the means to stay in their new homes, but nine times out of ten times, they didn't.

Big Mike just couldn't understand how people could look at the same numbers he was looking at and come to a completely different conclusion! He rationalized that people only see what they want to see. Hence his trepidation in making emotional decisions.

"Numbers don't lie!" Big Mike had yelled one night when he had been particularly upset that one of his best friends—with whom he'd taken the time to work out the numbers on financing a new business—went ahead and did it anyway despite Big Mike's protests that the friend could not afford it.

Grandpa John never understood either why people listened to their emotions rather than common-sense, clear-as-day projections that predicted exactly when they wouldn't be able to continue making their finance payments.

HAPPY RETURNS

Grandpa paid the first-year premium of $348,000.

What's the main point here? The premiums and the return?

Yes. Grandpa benefitted from greater leverage. The $348,000 that was safely invested in treasuries earning less than 3 percent now controlled a potential $4 million asset for the first thirteen years.

CHAPTER 6
LIFE GOES ON

Life sure wasn't as much fun after Grandpa John passed away. I just couldn't get used to the fact that he was really gone. At least once a week, I had a question regarding a business deal that I wanted to ask him about—only to realize that he wouldn't be able to answer my questions anymore.

Grandpa John had been a larger-than-life personality. Everyone who knew him thought of him as a dear friend. He knew how to have a good time, and he had a big, booming, infectious laugh that couldn't help but make you smile. He was truly beloved by his family, friends, and the community—a fact evidenced by the number of people who showed up for his funeral. Everyone missed him.

But it was Grandma who missed him the most. The first time I ever saw her cry was at his funeral. They had just celebrated their fifty-fifth wedding anniversary and were getting ready to travel around as much of the world as they could. Unfortunately, Grandpa John passed right before they were supposed to leave.

At first, Grandma handled everything remarkably well. The perfect partner and loving wife—so devoted, beautiful, and surprisingly funny—was remarkably strong until the realization that her beloved husband, best friend, and soul mate was gone. Grandpa John had been her whole world—and she his—and now she was alone in a new world without her partner.

However, she didn't sit around and feel sorry for herself for long. She persevered like a hardened soldier. I like to think Grandpa John would've been extremely proud of her.

The Sunday after Grandpa John's funeral, Big Mike gathered the family for a brief announcement. He cleared his throat, of course, and then proceeded to thank me for letting our family be prepared for Grandpa John's passing. As difficult as it had been on everyone, there was a silver lining. Grandpa John's dream of leaving a legacy for future generations of our family who wanted to start, grow, or expand a business were succeeding beyond his wildest dreams.

Grandpa John and Grandma had decided to transfer the ownership of the policy on Grandma's $4 million life insurance policy to Big Mike and Mom. When she passed away, they would not be subject to any income and estate taxes beyond the standard three-year transfer period. All the policy options were transferred to Big Mike and Mom.

As for Grandma, she collected the benefit from Grandpa John's policy and then lived comfortably by herself until she passed away quietly in her sleep.

She was eighty-eight years old.

After Grandma's death, the $4 million death benefit was paid to Big Mike and Mom.

TOTAL PREMIUMS PAID

Age		Premiums
69	Year 1 Premium:	$348,000
70–80	Premiums:	$0.00
81–88	Total Premiums:	$720,000
Total Premiums Paid:		$1,068,000

RETURN ON PREMIUMS PAID

Death Benefit Paid:	$4,000,000
Less Premiums Paid:	$1,068,000
Net Return:	$2,932,000
Internal Rate of Return:	11.02%
Tax Equivalent Return:	18.18%*

*What you would need to earn in a taxable account to net 11.02% in the 35% federal tax bracket.

CHAPTER 7
THE 2-FOR-1 STRATEGY

When Grandpa John and Grandma were alive, I had sat down with them and Big Mike to review their two original policies. I had wanted them to know about a new strategy I had been helping clients purchase for their own financial portfolios—something I called my "*two lives are better than one*" strategy.

Big Mike and I spent hours reviewing the complicated formulas behind this "2-for-1 strategy." My belief was that we could figure out a way to drive the cost of the insurance premiums down by 20 or 30 percent, and increase the death benefit payoff. Near the end of our number-crunching session, Big Mike asked me, "If it works so well and so inexpensively on one life, then why wouldn't it be up to twice as effective on two people?"

I knew Big Mike's question had been driven by logic. He was forever searching his beloved numbers for a statistical advantage that he could exploit. The fact was that the odds of one of the two people insured living longer was higher than if only one person were insured. Therefore, the cost of insurance was reduced. So we set about trying to determine how much an insurance premium would decrease if we insured Grandpa John and Grandma for the same $4 million policy instead of insuring them separately.

SURVIVORSHIP LIFE INSURANCE

This strategy is unfortunately entitled a "survivorship" or "second-to-die" policy. I know, it's tacky and more than a little insensitive, but it's a relic from a different era. And hey, at least it's not as bad as the ridiculously named "death benefit"! Talk about something that desperately needs to be renamed and rebranded . . . why couldn't they call it a "lifetime payoff" instead?

To this day, I'm sure there are thousands, if not tens of thousands or even hundreds of thousands, of people who don't seriously consider buying any life insurance because of scary-sounding policies that conjure up fear and suspicion instead of security and serenity. But that's a different battle for a different day.

The "second-to-die" policy acquired its unfortunate nickname because it accurately describes the policy, which is payable upon the death of the surviving spouse. Insuring two lives instead of one reduces the premiums by as much as 30 percent. In other words, if the policy is 30 percent less expense up front, then the tax-free rate of return could be just as competitive or better as a policy on just one life.

Realizing this, Big Mike asked, "How much are the premiums on a $4 million policy on two lives, ages sixty-nine and sixty-eight?" (Grandpa John was sixty-nine at the time, and Grandma was sixty-eight.)

I gave him two options:

POLICY DESIGN A

Pay annual premiums of $54,319 per year for the same $4 million. Keep in mind that the annual premiums on Grandpa John were $94,839 and Grandma's were $82,442 for the same $4 million benefit. You can look at the comparable rates of return and see that after the early years, the returns become pretty close.

POLICY DESIGN B

For example, take a look at the numbers I've compiled below and pay particular attention to the fact that we put more money in during year one, but the policy had no premiums in years two, three, four, five, six, seven, eight, nine, ten, eleven, twelve, thirteen, fourteen, and fifteen.

That's fourteen years with no premiums! And when the premiums begin again—if they even do—they're just $85,000 per year, or 2.1 percent of the death benefit.

That rate is locked in because it's a "guaranteed policy"—the premium will never go up or down, and the policyholder will never have to pay more than 2.1 percent of the death benefit. The policyholder would have to pay almost forty-three annual premium payments at 2.1 percent beginning at age eighty-four to equal the $4 million to break even, including the $395,591 first-year premium. Do the math . . . at that time he or she would be well over 120. That is not very likely to happen.

In Option B, you warehouse $395,591 up front, which carries the policy through year fifteen with no premiums. In Option A, you pay the $54,319 annually, and fifteen years later, you have paid a total of $814,785. That's $419,194 more premiums over the same period as Option B.

Grandpa John and Grandma Survivorship (Second-to-Die) Policy Example Comparison of $4 Million Annual Pay and Creative Premium Pay Policies					
(Option A) Annual Premiums				(Option B) Creative Design	
Yr	Age	Premiums	IRR	Premiums	IRR
1	69	$54,319	7,263.91%	$395,591	911.15%
2	70	$54,319	709.59%	$0	217.99%
3	71	$54,319	281.01%	$0	116.24%
4	72	$54,319	161.03%	$0	78.32%
5	73	$54,319	108.39%	$0	58.84%
6	74	$54,319	79.69%	$0	47.05%
7	75	$54,319	61.90%	$0	39.17%
8	76	$54,319	49.92%	$0	33.54%
9	77	$54,319	41.37%	$0	29.31%
10	78	$54,319	34.99%	$0	26.03%
11	79	$54,319	30.07%	$0	23.41%
12	80	$54,319	26.17%	$0	21.26%
13	81	$54,319	23.02%	$0	19.48%
14	82	$54,319	20.42%	$0	17.97%
15	83	$54,319	18.26%	$0	16.68%
16	84	$54,319	16.42%	$85,000	15.38%
17	85	$54,319	14.85%	$85,000	14.22%
18	86	$54,319	13.49%	$85,000	13.18%
19	87	$54,319	12.30%	$85,000	12.23%
20	88	$54,319	11.26%	$85,000	11.37%
21	89	$54,319	10.35%	$85,000	10.57%
22	90	$54,319	9.53%	$85,000	9.84%
Life Expectancy 22 years at origination					
23	91	$54,319	8.80%	$85,000	9.16%
24	92	$54,319	8.14%	$85,000	8.53%
25	93	$54,319	7.55%	$85,000	7.94%
26	94	$54,319	7.01%	$85,000	7.40%
27	95	$54,319	6.53%	$85,000	6.88%
28	96	$54,319	6.08%	$85,000	6.40%
29	97	$54,319	5.67%	$85,000	5.95%

Grandpa John and Grandma Survivorship (Second-to-Die) Policy Example Comparison of $4 Million Annual Pay and Creative Premium Pay Policies					
(Option A) Annual Premiums				**(Option B) Creative Design**	
Yr	Age	Premiums	IRR	Premiums	IRR
30	98	$54,319	5.30%	$85,000	5.53%
31	99	$54,319	4.95%	$85,000	5.13%
32	100	$54,319	4.63%	$85,000	4.75%
Total Premiums:		**$1,738,208**		**$1,840,591**	

Looking at it another way, we see that the life insurance company passes along a $419,194 discount in the first fifteen years—almost 50 percent—for warehousing a lump sum of cash up front.

Making money is all in the math.

In Option B, startup premiums (annual premiums that begin again after a number of years of zero premium payments) begin in year sixteen and Big Mike and Mom's joint life expectancy for their current ages is twenty-two years.

With such a policy, you select your design based on the facts, goals, and objectives. The insurance company provides enormous flexibility. Some people will take advantage of the options and some won't. You select your design based on your cash flow, goals, and objectives within the parameters outlined, and the life insurance company delivers a final contract tailored to you and your family or business.

Everyone wins when you understand the math!

To keep the second-to-die life insurance policy out of their estate—so the death benefit could be received income- and estate-tax-free—Grandpa John and Grandma instructed Big Mike and Mom to purchase the policy so they would be both owners and beneficiaries. In turn, they made cash gifts to Big Mike and Mom so they could pay the premiums. Simple, yet effective.

How many annual gifts of $13,000 per person can Grandpa John and Grandma both gift annually under current tax law? They can each use their $13,000 tax-free annual gifts to as many people as they desire. If we made them for our family—Big Mike and Mom, my three brothers and me, our wives, and the twelve grandkids—that would total twenty-two people who could receive $13,000 from both Grandpa and Grandma each year. That's a total nontaxable gift of up to $286,000 from Grandpa John and $286,000 from Grandma, totaling $572,000. That money could be used for the payment of life insurance premiums. Remember, if they had not gifted the dollars during their lifetime, the money would have been caught in their estate and taxed at up to 35 percent, turning every dollar into approximately sixty-five cents after estate tax.

On December 17, 2010, President Obama signed a new tax bill into law that reinstates the federal estate tax as a maximum of 35 percent and an estate tax exemption of $5 million.

PART 2

KNOW YOUR OPTIONS

CHAPTER 8

NEVER BE ASHAMED TO TAKE A PROFIT

A few weeks after Grandma passed, I was sitting at the kitchen table with my parents. Mom was drowning her French toast in an ocean of syrup, and Big Mike was coating his toast with powdered sugar with the skill of an artist stroking a canvas.

Something about watching my parents go about their everyday rituals made me smile. I was reminded of how far my family had come. Maybe it was the nice house I was sitting in—or the contentment and happiness that radiated from Big Mike and Mom, who were so obviously in love that strangers often thought they were newlyweds!

As I looked around the house at the rows and rows of family pictures of my brothers and their respective families, I was struck again with profound appreciation and gratitude for my Grandpa John.

His focused determination and unsurpassed work ethic had created fifty-five auto lube franchises in seventeen different states, ultimately allowing him to create a legacy for our entire family that could be passed on for generations. I was enormously proud to have helped Grandpa John contribute to that legacy by designing the life insurance strategy that created a gross return of $12 million dollars of tax-free cash to our family—all accomplished in a relatively short time, without breaking a sweat or lifting a shovel.

In fact, the most we did was create a new family motto to live by: "Make the most money, warehouse the least amount of money—and then *pass it on!*"

Considering the spectacular returns we made, the premiums my family paid were the wisest money we ever spent. We had not assumed any unnecessary risk; in fact, we came to realize that investment-grade life insurance was one of the safest financial purchases we—or anyone— could ever make.

Big Mike and my brothers were in total awe of the financial power they had discovered in the misunderstood investment-grade asset called life insurance. Like many others, they came to see that stocks cannot provide you with that tax-free power, and neither can bonds or real estate.

Only life insurance can be customized and strategically tailored to your family's unique situation. Only life insurance can provide tax-free returns on your premiums that often exceed 300 percent to 500 percent or more on premiums paid.

Investment-grade life insurance does all this—and it doesn't have the inherent risks that other assets do. It doesn't constantly fluctuate like the stock market. You don't need to check the paper every morning or your wireless device to see how much money you made or lost that day.

Investment-grade life insurance doesn't go through boom and bust cycles like some other riskier investments. It is not market correlated. You'll never pay more for a strategically designed life insurance policy than it's worth—or be forced to keep paying for it because you're locked in and don't have a choice.

And, as you get older and your financial situation changes, you can generally restructure the policies to better align with your objectives and financial status. In many cases, lowering the death benefit along with annual premiums are an option as well as pulling out cash or even exchanging your existing policy for a newer, better-performing policy.

The real beauty of life insurance is that it's scalable. Life insurance companies set guidelines for the death benefit amount they will allow you to buy based on your net worth. That's called your life insurance "capacity." Anyone who qualifies can buy it—and everyone can benefit from it. It's the most accessible asset I've ever found to help build a family's net worth, regardless of whether it's $100,000 or $1 billion.

CHAPTER 9
THE CHALLENGE

I guess you could say that, in my family, I'm the one with the mathematical expertise and experience in the life insurance industry. But let's face it, Big Mike calls the shots. As for Mom? Well, Mom had never said much on the subject, but that was about to change.

How did I know? She was sitting at the table eating breakfast with us. That's something she had not done since Taylor, her prized brown and tan beagle, went missing. So I knew she had something on her mind.

With Mom, there were never any mathematical calculations, spreadsheets, or flowcharts. She had no love for numbers like Big Mike and me. What she did have was a truly uncommon common sense and intuition that was spookily accurate. She could sense exaggeration from a mile away. She also had a profound moral compass that guided everything she did; if something were not the "right thing to do," she simply wouldn't do it.

So I was a bit surprised (and secretly delighted) when Mom pushed her French toast aside and said, "My dad is seventy-seven, and his goals for life insurance have changed, and that will impact our ability to pay the annual premiums. We need to make a decision about whether to continue the life insurance policy we bought on him and my mom."

Seventeen years earlier, Big Mike and Mom had purchased a survivorship life insurance policy, with a death benefit of $10 million on her parents. Grandpa Fred and Terry had both been sixty years old at the time. Remember that survivorship, or second-to-die policies, pay at the second death and can have up to 30 percent or so cheaper annual premiums than individual policies require.

Twelve years after they bought the policy, Terry passed away from thyroid cancer. Grandpa Fred had been living on his own ever since and only recently seemed to be finally settling down without her. I guess after forty-three years of marriage, that was to be expected.

Grandpa Fred had been a successful man in his own right, although he liked to play down his success. He had invested in real estate and simply sold to the highest bidder. He frequently referred to his success as "dumb luck." For instance, when he made an enormous profit on a property sale, he simply shrugged his shoulders and said, "Even a blind squirrel eventually finds an acorn."

Grandpa Fred might have projected a self-deprecating image, but truth be told, he was a shrewd investor with a real gift for identifying properties that were undervalued. My favorite example of this gift was his purchase of the deserted parking lot in a blighted area ridden with crime and homeless people. He took a lot of grief from Mom and everyone else for buying it. But he knew something we didn't know: the land would one day be worth something. And he was right. Years after he sold the land, the professional football team built its $1.5 billion stadium there.

So when Mom posed the question of what to do with Grandpa Fred's policy, Big Mike responded with one of his own: "Well, what do you have in mind?"

Mom didn't answer at first. She paused for a moment, and then calmly said, "We've been so blessed, but times are changing. My dad has decided to make some serious changes to his estate plan that will eliminate the annual gift we receive and use to pay the annual premiums on the $10 million policy."

She paused again, drew a long breath, and then continued. "It's not clear what we are going to do with the policy, but why don't you prepare our best available options to see if we can find some opportunity in this sudden chaos."

Big Mike wasted no time. The breakfast dishes were not even cleared from the table before he asked me to dig out the $10 million life insurance policy on Grandpa Fred.

CHAPTER 10
THE DESIGN IS THE GENIUS

When you design a life insurance policy, you need to think like a casino owner in Las Vegas: you're "the house" and you set the odds. You design the policy within the guidelines set forth by the life insurance companies. You have a hand in setting the direction for the entire outcome, from beginning to end.

With that in mind, let's see how Grandpa Fred and Terry's policy actually performed seventeen years later.

The writing agent at the time the policy was purchased was my mentor, Jack Freidman. What most people don't understand about life insurance policies is that each policy contains the same standard features. That is, every agent receives the same template.

An agent can input the same standard items, such as name, health rating, age, and death benefit amount, and then just press a button and the mathematical illustration pops up, showing the annual premiums to be paid for the death benefit amount desired.

Now, in some cases that's okay. I'm just really passionate about how important it is for your investment-grade life insurance policy to be customized for your family's particular needs.

I just don't believe that the first interaction or interview with an interested client should consist of a few basic questions that, when answered and entered into the big life insurance agency software programs, quickly spits out the policy just like that.

That's not only a bad way to buy life insurance, it's also a pretty bad way to buy just about anything.

Think about it. If you were adding a new addition to your home, would you approve the first plan presented to you and then sign the first loan offered? No, of course, you wouldn't. You would do some due diligence.

Designing a life insurance strategy that is worthy of a position in your financial portfolio is like designing a new addition to your home. There are lots of creative decisions to be made to get the best results.

Have you ever seen a magic trick revealed? What happens the next time you see the same trick? No magic, right?

Essentially, I pulled back the curtain and showed my family the actual mathematics—the nuts and bolts of the design on Grandpa Fred's policy. I showed them how to design a policy structure where you bet you are going to live instead of die, and make money with the life insurance company.

It's my version of *The Emperor Has No Clothes*.

Why not diversify your portfolio with an investment-grade life insurance policy that can work many ways for you and your family—whether you are alive or dead?

Once you connect the formulas with the basic numbers/math behind a successful strategy, you can take greater control to optimize your results. That's how successful people have been trained.

Purchasing life insurance buys you far more than peace of mind. It guarantees that you and your spouse, children, and estate will be far wealthier than if you hadn't purchased the policy.

What other asset functions as a *wealth accumulation tool, growing your cash within the policy tax free, allowing you to borrow money out tax free along the way, and paying a tax-free benefit at completion?* Oh, and did I mention that it is not market correlated? That is does not fluctuate wildly with the up-and-down economic cycles of the global economy?

Only investment-grade life insurance.

It works when you're not working—twenty-four hours a day, seven days a week, three hundred and sixty-five days a year. This market never closes.

The way insurance companies formulate the policies and structure the premiums for each customer is all based on mathematical formulas. To get the best design, many times you can do a whole lot more than punch in your age, sex, health rating, and death benefit. You have to think like the "house."

So, how could you possibly better your results?

You won't unless you're willing to think, act, and—for all intents and purposes—become the "house" yourself.

To do that requires a radical readjustment of your mindset. It requires a new way of looking at familiar problems so you're able to reframe the age-old questions and provide logical, profitable solutions for you and your family.

Remember, the "house" is bound by the odds and formulas upon which it has flourished for so long. You can have just as much success, but it won't always be as easy as simply paying your premium on time—or, as you've seen, premiums you don't pay.

Sometimes, like with Grandpa Fred, life on life's terms can force you to adapt to unforeseen circumstances and unpredictable outcomes.

If you logically conclude, based on the formulas I've shown you, that your return on the investment window is shrinking, then continue working the mathematical options.

Trust me, if you don't educate yourself, do your homework, and find an agent you can trust who knows the math and the rules, then you are setting yourself up for a mistake—a mistake will only get more and more expensive.

However, if you open yourself up to possibility thinking, then you can position yourself to profit whenever possible.

Knowledge is power. That's why we hire top CPAs, architects, surgeons, coaches, and professionals in all fields. In life insurance, knowledge is demonstrated in the final policy design. Passion is knowledge on fire. You need to constantly research and explore every option to maximize your profits—just like the "house." My mentor, Jack Freidman, retired comfortably and is now playing golf in Naples, Florida. I was fortunate to ride his coattails for almost ten years, consuming his creative ideas and expanding on the mathematical possibilities for each and every client.

CHAPTER 11

MAKE MONEY BUYING LIFE INSURANCE

It happens all the time. Clients come to me who don't have enough insurance, don't have their policies reviewed regularly, and don't understand the compelling value proposition in this asset called life insurance. I'm forced to reposition life insurance as a profitable asset— explain to them that it turns into *cash*—so they begin to pay closer attention and make sound business decisions.

I don't understand why policyholders surrender or quit before their policies pay out. Life insurance companies give consumers an exhausting array of options to help people maintain their policies. They can reduce the death benefit, give you cash back, exchange the policy to a lower-premium policy, or uncover the tremendous tax-free benefits buried in the policy—just to name a few options.

Let me repeat what I just said: life insurance pays off in *cash*!

Wouldn't you like to purchase life insurance and get one of the most cost-efficient policies with one of the highest possible rates of returns?

Of course you would. Yet countless people surrender or quit. They make life insurance decisions in a vacuum when they should be making sound business decisions.

Simply put, life insurance is a formula, and formulas don't make exceptions. But just as my good friend and former insurance partner Randy Perkins says, "Bad information leads to bad decisions." The good news is that good information can lead to good decisions, and great information is the way to know you've made a good choice.

When I design a policy, I try to customize it for my particular client's needs instead of using the standard template. I make it work by computing potentially hundreds of variables such as health, premiums, catch-ups, companies, ratings, cost, fees, and so forth. Only then do I get one of the most efficient and effective personalized policy designs.

The goal is to build profitable mathematical options and advantages into the policy based on the client's own health rating, goals, and objectives.

So with that in mind, let's review Grandpa Fred's $10 million policy. When they purchased the policy seventeen years ago, Grandpa Fred and Terry were rated "preferred health," which resulted in an annual premium of $83,242. That is exactly the amount that Grandpa Fred gifted our family each year to make the premiums. After seventeen years, the total premiums paid totaled $1,415,114.

Grandpa Fred – Preferred Health – $10 Million – 17 Years after Inception				
Yr	End of Yr Age	Premium Outlay	Net Death Benefit (DB)	Internal Rate of Return (IRR) on DB
17	77	$83,242	$10,000,000	19.47%
Total premiums paid thru year 17 total $1,415,114.				
18	78	$83,242	$10,000,000	17.83%
19	79	$83,242	$10,000,000	16.41%
20	80	$83,242	$10,000,000	15.15%
21	81	$83,242	$10,000,000	14.04%
22	82	$83,242	$10,000,000	13.05%
23	83	$83,242	$10,000,000	12.17%
24	84	$83,242	$10,000,000	11.37%
25	85	$83,242	$10,000,000	10.65%
26	86	$83,242	$10,000,000	10.00%

Yr	End of Yr Age	Premium Outlay	Net Death Benefit (DB)	Internal Rate of Return (IRR) on DB
	Grandpa Fred – Preferred Health – $10 Million – 17 Years after Inception			
27	87	$83,242	$10,000,000	9.41%
28	88	$83,242	$10,000,000	8.86%
29	99	$83,242	$10,000,000	8.36%
30	90	$83,242	$10,000,000	7.91%
31	91	$83,242	$10,000,000	7.48%
32	92	$83,242	$10,000,000	7.09%
33	93	$83,242	$10,000,000	6.73%
34	94	$83,242	$10,000,000	6.39%
35	95	$83,242	$10,000,000	6.08%
36	96	$83,242	$10,000,000	5.78%
37	97	$83,242	$10,000,000	5.51%
38	98	$83,242	$10,000,000	5.25%
39	99	$83,242	$10,000,000	5.01%
40	100	$83,242	$10,000,000	4.78%

The most important variable we needed to factor in was the unknown—the "what if?" component. "What if I can't make the premiums in the future?" "What if I want to bail out?" It's always best to manage your risk as best you can. But life comes at you on life's terms, and you never know what's going to happen. You can be prepared if you plan wisely enough. So in our family's case, what if Big Mike and Mom, who owned the policy, suddenly had to bail out?

I had to obey my what-if variable, which in this case, was the cash-surrender value in year seventeen of $1,315,294.

My family paid in $1,415,114 over seventeen years and had a bailout cash surrender value of $1,315,294.

That's 93 percent of their money after seventeen years controlling $10 million!

Where can you control so much potential cash for so little, quit after seventeen years, and still get 93 cents on the dollar when you bail out?

Remember, during all that time the "house" has been on the hook for $10 million.

After seventeen years, Big Mike and Mom are out of pocket only $99,820, or $5,871 per year for $10,000,000, tax free ($1,415,114 - $1,315,294 = $99,820). It's absurd to think that the consumer can control so much for so little.

Did Big Mike and Mom want their $1,315,294 cash back or the $10 million benefit? Of course they wanted the $10 million, but what appeared to be a simple answer became a lot more complicated based on life's unexpected challenges.

CHAPTER 12

IF THE MATH WORKS . . . DO IT

Big Mike and Mom own a $10 million life insurance policy on Grandpa Fred and Terry. Since Terry passed away, technically the policy is just on Grandpa Fred, with the annual premium calculated at the discounted rate for two people.

However, that annual premium is $83,242. And that is causing concern for Big Mike. Like everyone else, he has seen the economies of the richest countries in the world brought to a scary, screeching halt.

A global recession threatens to become a global depression. It's the worst financial crisis since the Great Depression. The fluctuation in the market is driving investors away in droves, and people everywhere are stockpiling cash and trying to sell assets and increase cash flow.

Big Mike had been concerned about interest rates and the economy. For some time now, he and Mom had been seriously considering surrendering and cashing in their $10 million policy. They just did not want the $83,242 annual premium obligation.

I couldn't believe—nor did I understand—Big Mike's reasoning. This man who was usually obsessed with the logic and purity of numbers was letting his emotions cloud his judgment.

"You bought the policy on Grandpa Fred for the long haul," I said. "Remember our strategy? Think like the 'house'?"

I could see that Big Mike was trying to think of a defense, but nothing came out of his mouth.

So I continued my press. "Would the house *ever* fold when it knew it had the best hand?" I argued. "No way! And we're not going to either."

I continued my rant until finally Big Mike relented. And then I continued on some more for good measure.

I reinforced my sermon, stating that the person who goes the distance and collects the death benefit makes the most money. I said, "Getting out early reduces your opportunity for the big return—and that's why we bought the policy. That was the goal. Why would we cut and run now when after seventeen years, the payoff is getting closer and not farther away?"

Big Mike remained silent.

"Worst case, you bail out and collect the $1,315,294 cash surrender value in the life insurance policy. Not bad—but not good for a consolation prize on $10 million tax free down the road!"

Big Mike had heard enough. He turned to me and made a simple statement: "Grandpa Fred has decided to gift 100 percent of his estate to his and Terry's favorite charities. In turn, there is no need for the $10 million of life insurance to pay the inheritance tax anymore, because there is no inheritance. Bottom line, there will be no more annual gifts from Grandpa Fred to pay the premiums on the $10 million policy. So Mom and I have decided to raise cash, and raise it quickly."

"It's a $10 million policy, Dad!" I yelled. "Just do the math! Go the distance!"

I stopped my rant, wondering if perhaps I was the one who was thinking a little too emotionally. I decided I was and stomped, rather dramatically, outside for a breath of fresh air.

CHAPTER 13
PUT IT IN PERSPECTIVE

Let's look at the value proposition for Grandpa Fred's policy.
It's hard to understand the value until you compare it to today's replacement cost.

So that's what we are going to do. What would the cost be on the policy Big Mike and Mom bought on Grandpa Fred and Terry seventeen years ago be today?

Annual Premiums for $10 Million Policy	Annual Premium	% Increase
1. Current policy bought seventeen years ago:	$83,242 per year	Base
2. New permanent policy if bought today:	$539,935 per year	648%
3. Ten-year term insurance if bought today:	$375,160 per year	450%

Let's recap the severe penalties they would have paid if they had waited until today to purchase the policy:

1. The current policy Big Mike and Mom own started out as a survivorship policy on two lives, which made the premiums cheaper than buying a policy on one life. The life expectancy of two healthy people is always longer than one. They benefited with a premium from inception at age sixty that was almost 30 percent cheaper than buying insurance on just one person. Terry passed, and the fact that Big Mike and Mom bought the policy on Grandpa Fred and Terry seventeen years ago—when they were younger, in better health, and rates were cheaper—gave them a decisive low-cost advantage, which delivered more potential upside return.

   Big Mike and Mom have paid $1,415,114 over seventeen years and have a bailout cash surrender value of $1,315,294.

2. If Big Mike and Mom were to buy a new permanent life policy on Grandpa Fred today, the premium would be $539,935 per year. In three years, they would pay over $1.6 million in premiums, which is higher than they have paid in seventeen years with the original policy. In addition, there is a zero cash surrender value in the new policy if they quit!

3. Cheap-term insurance qualifies as "the benchmark" in the life insurance industry, delivering the lowest cost for a preset period of time only.

   A ten-year level term insurance quote is about $375,160 per year, if you can even buy it. It takes only four years of paying the $375,160 in annual premiums, totaling $1,500,640, to surpass what Big Mike and Mom paid in the entire seventeen years they have owned the original policy.

Now here's the clincher: if Grandpa Fred's health changes, he could become *uninsurable* at any price!

You buy life insurance when you are healthy because when your health changes for the worse—which is inevitable over time—the cost of insurance rates increase, lowering your internal rate of return (IRR). You could even be uninsurable! That's exactly when you want to own the maximum amount of life insurance the insurance companies will sell you because you may never again qualify to buy it!

What you already own is priceless!

CHAPTER 14
MY ICEBERG THEORY

You remember the *Titanic*. It hit an iceberg and tragically sank, taking more than 1,500 people with it. The ship's crew did what they could to avoid the iceberg—the part they could see. As we all know, the iceberg you see above water is not the real danger, is it? It's what you don't or cannot see that hurts you.

When I began this process, I primarily wanted to dispel the myth of what life insurance wasn't—a bill or a nuisance. I thought I could then help people alter or change the negative behavior patterns associated with buying/acquiring/maintaining large amounts of life insurance that they previously knew almost nothing about.

Basically, most people outside of the life insurance business know absolutely, positively nothing about it. That's as in zilch, zero, nada—yet tens and hundreds of millions of people own life insurance products and annuities.

People just know that they have it or they don't. And then there are some who used to have it, but quit.

Whatever you thought about life insurance before, try to forget it. I want to help you re-imagine the entire process.

The challenge before us isn't small; in fact, it's enormous and all encompassing.

Before I reveal the steps I take to lead curious prospective clients not yet committed toward considering restructuring their current life insurance policy into a fully customized investment-grade life insurance policy, I will say this. While the vast majority of my clientele belong in the upper income bracket's top percentile, it's entirely *not* true that you must be rich to follow the policies and techniques I present here.

Everything's scalable.

I have represented a wide range of wealthy people—from billionaires to millionaires to up-and-coming entrepreneurs—all of whom want the same things: to diversify their portfolio assets while they are still accumulating them and to increase their net worth.

The last few years in particular have seen a large shift of investors searching for real returns net of taxes, fees, and inflation. That search has opened the door to the life insurance experience—tailored to each business, entrepreneur, family, and charity. Life insurance is one of the best conservative-to-intermediate risk-versus-return vehicles offered in the global financial industry.

Remember earlier when I mentioned the propensity of wealthy families for deploying the most innovative financial tools and strategies to make even more money? The wealthy have always been the pied pipers when it comes to the latest innovations in the financial system. They have the resources to find innovation. One resource in particular presents them with numerous advantages—the priceless luxury of time.

Time, quite frankly, is on their side.

The wealthy can also afford to take bigger risks. Have you ever heard "the more your risk, the bigger your reward"?

My point in telling you about the majority of their incomes is simply this: Almost all of them are at or near the top of their chosen professions. They didn't get where they are by simply waiting for something to happen to them. To get where they are, they had to prove themselves every day in every way at every level.

And once they got to the top? Was it time to kick off their shoes and relax by being passive or not engaging at the start of each meeting? No.

When I've asked potential clients how much life insurance they own, these normally charismatic captains of industry, these phenomenally successful men and women, get defensive.

That might be my fault, actually.

I have to tell these incredibly gifted, smart, successful people that they haven't acted at all like the incredibly gifted, smart, successful people they are.

When people end up in my office, it is usually because they suspect they might have made some mistakes—mistakes that are getting more and more expensive.

So I'll ask a simple question: "Is it safe to say you didn't completely understand what you were buying when you bought your life insurance policy?"

They typically nod their heads.

"How much life insurance would you buy if life insurance had a net-zero cost?" I ask.

I always know the answer.

"Well, as much as I possibly could!" Just like Grandpa John.

"And is it also fair to say that you bought a small amount because you don't completely understand it—and don't like paying for it?" I ask.

And there's the breakthrough. A light bulb goes on when they realize they really would buy as much as they could at a net-zero cost. They just don't like paying for it! Sound familiar?

Now we are ready to move forward with a little mathematical recap that leads to the traditional business decision-making process again, which is where they find their comfort zone.

CHAPTER 15

INVESTMENT-GRADE OR TRADITIONAL LIFE INSURANCE?

Big Mike always taught us to always to tell the truth, even when revealing it might be uncomfortable or awkward. Even when the truth might hurt someone.

"Better to be hurt by truth than wounded by silence," he rationalized.

Big Mike believed you hurt someone far more by keeping quiet and pretending there wasn't anything wrong. He also knew that there weren't too many people left these days who had the courage or the conviction to stick with being truthful; he felt that most people just tell you what they think you want to hear.

The truth behind why you didn't purchase as much life insurance as you can afford or qualify for isn't complex.

Perhaps you simply didn't completely understand the value proposition of what you were buying. Perhaps you weren't in the right frame of mind. Perhaps you were not prepared to assimilate the facts and make a well-informed financial decision.

Life insurance turns into large amounts of cash. There are financial opportunities when you understand the rules of the game and what is at stake. The last thing you want to be is at a tremendous financial disadvantage—in any business or any financial situation.

Can you imagine going to a casino where the dealer not only knows your hand, but he also knows exactly how you'll play it?

It's practically *impossible* for the house to lose.

And why shouldn't it be? That is how a casino builds a rock-solid business that can pay big money when you finally hit a winning streak.

Casinos have been winning for so long now that it's just accepted as fact. We've become so docile and obedient as a society that we just accept whatever we're told is the industry standard.

Let me make one thing clear. I'm not advocating rejecting anything. Nor am I telling you to be hyper-vigilant because corporations only exist to break the backs of the common man.

That kind of thinking is extreme nonsense. Corporations depend on their brands being respected and held in the highest regard by every race, class, and creed.

That said, these aren't exactly neighborhood mom-and-pop businesses anymore.

Many life insurance companies have either become domestic or multinational global conglomerates themselves. Some have even made the leap from mutual insurance companies owned by policyholders to publicly traded companies listed on their respective stock exchanges.

The contemporary corporate culture thrives on "informational" advantages, which has the leading product, marketing, and distribution edge to better serve customers—and find new ones—than at any other time in their fantastically successful history.

But when you assume life insurance is the same product it's always been, when you don't perform the same due diligence that you wouldn't think twice about if you were about to buy a 50-unit apartment complex—you've set yourself up for failure because both can be worth millions. Whether it's real estate or life insurance, it's all green—it's cash and it spends the same.

You'll meet with an agent maybe once or twice, get an insurance-approved doctor to give you a physical, and then, after your agent has captured the relevant data, you'll watch the agent plug your most relevant physical and lifestyle characteristics into the formula that generations of insurance agents and life insurance conglomerates have been tweaking for the last century. The fantastically dependable template.

But if you only knew what the dealer knew . . .

And now you do. The secret is in your health rating and policy illustration design—and the possibility that up to 88 percent of permanent policyowners quit their policies. What does that really mean to you? How can you use that profound knowledge to profit? The answer is short and sweet. If it really is true that up to 88 percent quit, that means one out of eight people actually do go the distance. Stated another way, seven of eight quit, and those seven who quit help subsidize the one that goes the distance by allowing him or her affordable premiums that may not have been even remotely possible.

Be the one, not the seven.

FINAL DECISION

Ultimately, Big Mike and Mom exercised their option to cash in and take the surrender value of $1,315,294.

I was disappointed, but honestly, it was a very special moment for our family and I feel a little awkward even relaying the intimate details.

Suffice to say, it was a special day.

"The consumer is the winner again, right?" I joked, cracking a big smile while hugging my precious Mom. Their net cost out of pocket was only

$99,820 over seventeen years, or $5,871 per year, controlling a $10 million tax-free benefit. It almost sounds crazy to realize that the consumer ends up with so much for so little.

Before either Big Mike or I could say another word, Mom said, "We've been so fortunate. We won with a worst-case scenario, collecting $1.3 million. Now how bad can that really be?"

PART 3

MAKE MORE MONEY GIVING IT AWAY

CHAPTER 16
TURN $1.3 MILLION INTO $12 MILLION

Just when you thought things couldn't possibly get any better for my family, they did. A few months later, we learned a new way to create wealth and build our family legacy.

The entire family had gathered at my parents' home on New Year's Eve. We knew as soon as Big Mike started to clear his throat that something big was coming. We all leaned in and listened closely to what the gravelly voiced mathematical millionaire had to say.

"Boys, Mom and I acted impulsively in terminating the policy on Grandpa Fred and taking the $1.3 million cash," he admitted. Then he looked directly at me. "It was a mistake, and we are sorry we did not listen to you."

I nodded to him, grateful that he had finally come to understand what I had been so passionate about on that long-ago night. I was about to comment, but he stopped me. He was not done with the surprises.

"After a meaningful discussion, your Mom has come up with a plan that will affect our entire family," he said.

The plan was this: Mom was intent on helping others like us who were willing to work, so she wanted to take the $1.3 million we received from Grandpa Fred's policy and create a $12 million family legacy. The first step was to make a gift to a charity, the beginning of the "10-Bagger" strategy I had shared with Big Mike earlier and which he was now ready to unveil to the rest of the family.

Big Mike was intent on celebrating Mom's charitable stroke of genius. I had never seen her more animated in my life, and Big Mike was happy to let her soak up the spotlight that was usually reserved for him.

And it was right that she should have the spotlight. Although she was smart—she had finished college in three years—she had left the day-to-day bookkeeping to Big Mike. But when it came to the bigger financial decisions, she was right there by his side. They reached those decisions together.

I went over to Mom and gave her a huge hug, briefly lifting her petite body off the ground and hoisting her triumphantly in the air as my brothers began to chant "MOM! MOM! MOM!"

Mom laughed before shouting, "Put . . . me . . . down!"

I did, and when my brothers quieted down, I asked, "Hey Mom, before you spend that money, do you think you can finally go spend a little on yourself?"

"Oh, that's very thoughtful of you, David," she said. "But unless you know of something I'm in particular that I'm missing . . . "

And she left the end of the sentence hanging in midair. Typical Mom. That was all she was going to say on the subject of buying something for herself. I should've expected it. (And I should tell you that right then and there, I decided I'd take Big Mike and we'd get her something together.)

Big Mike tapped his glass again and again until our rowdy crowd quieted down.

"Mom has now set the bar pretty high in this family. I want to say something, and I want to say it now: we won again with life insurance. Now boys, that's how you buy life insurance and bet that you are going to live instead of die—and make money with the life insurance company!" he exclaimed.

Look at it this way: we had already made $12 million tax free from life insurance payouts.

Now they had just received another $1.3 million for the privilege of owning a $10 million policy for seventeen years. Sounds kind of strange, but that's the reality.

Another option would have been to gift the policy on Grandpa Fred and Terry, who had already passed, directly to charity and let the charity make the premiums and collect the death benefit, but that's not the way it all went down with the financial chaos that had surrounded Big Mike and Mom.

Needless to say, that weighed on Big Mike's mind when he presented the financial recap to the family. He wondered if he had made a mistake taking the cash surrender value versus holding on for $10 million. But, as the saying goes, what's done is done. Right?

Nope. I spoke too soon.

CHAPTER 17

THE "10-BAGGER" STRATEGY FOR CHARITY

What Big Mike and Mom were proposing was this: instead of taking the $1.3 million, they would instead donate the entire amount to charity on behalf of Grandpa Fred.

This $1.3 million gift to a qualified charity generated a 50 percent, or $650,000, tax deduction.

In turn, I would help the charity buy a second-to-die life insurance policy (a policy on the lives of Big Mike and Mom that pays off at the second death) for a single premium of $1.3 million in year one only.

Single premium meant not having to pay a premium ever again. That $1.3 million on Big Mike, age sixty, and Mom, who's a youthful fifty, buys a fully paid $12 million life insurance policy.

Ultimately, that's a payoff to the charity in excess of ten times the $1.3 million gift—and it also leaves Big Mike and Mom with a $650,000 tax deduction.

What charity would receive the donation? Well, Grandpa Fred had always talked about his beloved University of Redlands and its football program. Big Mike and Mom were in the position to make a gift to the university on his behalf, establishing a $12 million family legacy.

Who could've imagined that it was not only possible, but that you could actually make money . . . giving money away?

So how did they turn $1.3 million into $12 million? Let's do the math.

First, they paid in $1,415,114 over seventeen years, and then took the bailout and collected the cash surrender value of $1,315,294.

That's 93 percent of their money for owning a $10 million potential asset!

Using Mom's idea, they gifted the $1.3 million to Grandpa Fred's favorite college and received a $650,000 tax deduction.

The University of Redlands purchased a paid-up $12 million life insurance policy on Big Mike and Mom, adding $12 million to their endowment.

Everyone won!

The Sunday following the announcement, the president of the University of Redlands, Carrie Jensen, joined Grandpa Fred, Big Mike, and a perpetually smiling Mom, plus all my brothers, for our family dinner.

President Jensen was definitely a top-shelf guest. She chatted about Grandpa Fred's glory days at the U of R—particularly his junior year when he was a running back on the team that played for the national championship—and hit it off with everyone in the family, including my beagle, Lucky, who made himself at home and snuggled up against her feet under the dinner table.

President Jensen even gave the first toast of the evening: "I just want to take this time to recognize your touching generosity with the gift of $12 million donated to the university and the athletic department on behalf of Grandpa Fred. As a small token of our appreciation, the university has agreed to name the University of Redlands athletics field house after your family. On behalf of everyone at the university, and especially every student who will soon pass through the doors of this magnificent facility, we thank you for your bold, visionary gift to the U of R family."

She elegantly raised her glass into the air and toasted us. We were all profoundly moved by her speech, and then by her invitation to the entire family to attend the annual homecoming game. She revealed that Grandpa Fred would be recognized on the field as an honorary team captain during the game, walking with the other three team captains to the fifty-yard line for the opening coin toss.

Needless to say, Grandpa Fred was beyond proud.

Give $1.3 million to your favorite charity and then buy a life insurance policy at ten times that number. To them it's really the same as a $12 million gift.

The table below showcases the tax-free leverage that life insurance provides for different age groups. The example highlights a $10 million policy on both spouses who are the same age and same preferred health rating.

This illustration shows the one-pay premium for different couples' ages to leverage a gift of $10 million using life insurance.

$10 Million Survivorship Life Policy One-Pay Premium to Age 100			
	Ages	**One Pay**	**Return on $10 Million**
Male/Female	40/40	$514,413	19.4 to 1
Male/Female	50/50	$833,150	12 to 1
Male/Female	60/60	$1,367,729	7.3 to 1
Male/Female	70/70	$2,189,371	4.5 to 1
Male/Female	80/80	$3,214,135	3.1 to 1

I have also added a per-million illustration below so you can see how much a one-pay premium would be for two spouses/people of the same age with preferred health ratings to buy $1 million of survivorship life insurance. If you want to buy $2, $3, or $5 million, just multiply by that number. Of course, you can pay the premiums over any other period, such as five, ten, twenty, or more years.

	$1 Million Survivorship Life Policy One-Pay Premium to Age 100		
	Ages	One Pay	Return on $1 Million
Male/Female	40/40	$51,441	19.4 to 1
Male/Female	50/50	$83,315	12 to 1
Male/Female	60/60	$136,772	7.3 to 1
Male/Female	70/70	$218,937	4.5 to 1
Male/Female	80/80	$321,413	3.1 to 1

PART 4

NEVER PAY
TAXES AGAIN

CHAPTER 18

TAX-FREE RETIREMENT AT ANY AGE

Thanksgiving at our house was always a big deal.

We were the quintessential Italian-American family—big, boisterous, and always ready to celebrate the holidays with loved ones and friends. As the years passed, our celebrations grew even larger—our family was growing, as was our circle of friends and business partners, who were invited to join us as a gesture of appreciation for many blessings they had bestowed upon our family.

Of course, while the holidays were a time of joy, there was a bit of sadness, too. It wasn't an easy transition learning to live without our beloved Grandpa John, Grandma, and Terry. Their absences were felt the most during the holidays, particularly by Big Mike. He would get choked up when thinking of his parents, but in keeping with the old-school tough guy that he was, he'd gracefully slip out of the room when the emotions threatened to overcome him.

I think Big Mike's emotions during the holidays were borne of two thoughts: he was feeling nostalgic, obviously missing Grandpa John and Grandma, and deep down, I think he wished that his parents could've lived long enough to have seen his business boom.

Big Mike had always been successful. It was almost impossible for him not to be. He had one major philosophy that he credited with all of his success, something he had learned early in life. And that philosophy was to work hard and smart.

Big Mike had not been the fastest kid on the playground. He hadn't been the best athlete either. But he had been pretty good at everything he tried.

But for Big Mike, that wasn't enough. He had wanted to be great at something. He had tried pretty much everything he could—every sport, every after-school activity. He had even dabbled in the arts, learning to play instruments and trying his hand at acting and singing.

Then one day, one of those moments of clarity hit, forever shaping his view of success. A teacher mentioned to him that what he did best was try hard—that no student worked as hard as he did, and that if he continued to work harder and smarter than everyone else did, success would find him.

Big Mike took that teacher's words to heart, and from then on, he outworked everyone else. He was fond of saying that someone at a rival company might outtalk him, that a rival company might outbid him, but nobody would ever outwork him.

His unbeatable combination of a legendary work ethic, coupled with a street-smart business savvy, made Big Mike extremely successful. Of course, his uncanny mastery of mathematics, especially his savant-like ability to add large equations and figures instantly in his head, helped as well.

These character traits all helped shape him and his booming business. It was this knowledge—this power—that he wanted to share with all of us.

And so, about an hour before our Thanksgiving dinner, Mom tapped me on the shoulder and nodded down the hall to Big Mike's office.

I entered the room to find Big Mike with his arm around my brother Michael's shoulder. Michael was considered the brains in our family. He was a technology wizard who, after serving four years in the navy and graduating near the top of his class at Bentley College in Boston, filed and won approval for fourteen patents in computer science. And to think Big Mike had been worried about his future when his four-year hitch as a SeaBee ended!

While Michael was a genius with technology and computers, he was so focused on technology innovation that he never took the time to implement a strategy for managing any part of his own finances. Like most people, he had not invested the time necessary to master the financial world. But then, who does?

I happened to walk in the room right when Big Mike was saying how "smart your brother David is." I have to tell you that my chest swelled at that moment. I had not felt so good in months. Don't get me wrong, Big Mike had been very vocal about acknowledging my help in planning the family's financial legacy. But hearing him say I was smart to Michael, the real brains in the family, made it extra special.

In addition to getting an earful about me, Michael was also getting a hard sell from Big Mike on one of the policy designs that had brought me much personal financial success. When Big Mike noticed my presence in the room, he excitedly asked me to show Michael the *triple-tax-free* retirement strategy I'd been building into a number of my client's policies.

Of course, since Michael had spent almost all of his time in front of a computer creating patents, he had never been exactly focused on planning his financial future. It just was not a priority to him.

I could immediately tell from the look on his face that he was uncomfortable. I have seen this look on the faces on many clients. It means one thing: the client is about to leave. In Michael's case, he certainly would not dare walk out of Big Mike's office, but I knew that his mind could walk out of the conversation, and that was bad.

I knew I had to get to the point and emphasize the benefits fast.

"Hey, Michael, it's this simple," I said, snapping him back to attention with a quick clap of my hands. He responded quickly, his eyes turning to me.

"All you have to do is put the same amount of money away each year and forget about it," I told him.

He eyed me suspiciously. "That's all I have to do, and I'll never pay taxes on the growth of my money ever again?" he asked.

I nodded. Yup. That was all he had to do.

"Really?" Michael asked incredulously.

"That's it," I said, and then paused before adding, "Unless you want to do more."

"I'm not sure what I want to do," he replied. "Can you tell me a little more about what my options are?"

That was a great sign. Michael was acknowledging that he was out of his depth, in a place he didn't really understand and in which he wasn't entirely comfortable. Therefore, he was acting cautiously. I only wish more successful people had Michael's common sense.

"You want to make more money, right?" I asked.

"Sure. More money would be nice," he admitted.

I smiled. "Well, let's start with what a 'perfect' investment would look like, okay?"

"It doesn't have to be perfect. David," Michael replied.

"By 'perfect' I just mean the kind of things we'd be looking for if we were looking to make an investment," I said.

"Oh, okay. So you're teaching me the basics, right?" he asked.

"Exactly." I then explained that, ideally, the "perfect" investment would contain the following characteristics:

1. Tax-deductible contributions.

2. Tax deferral on growth.

3. Income-tax-free withdrawals.

4. Income-tax-free survivor benefits.

5. No plan administration fees.

6. No minimum or maximum contribution limits.

7. Owner decision about when to start withdrawals.

8. Cash liquidity in case of emergency.

9. Distribution amount flexibility at retirement.

10. Some protection from creditors.

11. A guarantee against investment losses.

"The perfect investment would mirror these eleven characteristics," I told Michael, "but with the federal government and many states combating major budget deficits at all levels, this 'perfect' investment doesn't exist."

"Bummer," replied Michael, sounding genuinely disappointed.

"However, with the proper investment-grade life insurance policy, you'll still be able to get ten out of those eleven characteristics."

Michael looked at my dad. "I can do that? Really?"

"Why do you think I had your mother go find David?" Big Mike replied. "I told you, your brother's got a gift for this kind of thing—a real gift!"

I jumped in before the bragging got out of hand. Michael was fully engaged in the conversation now, and I wanted to keep him that way. "The only gift I have is my obsessive, encyclopedia-like knowledge of the IRS code, and Internal Revenue Code Section 7702[1] helps us out

---

1 Policy Loans: Assuming the life insurance policy is not an MEC, policy loans from a life insurance policy are not treated as withdrawals or distributions and are not subject to income tax. IRC § 7702(f). Tax-free income assumes (1) withdrawals do not exceed tax basis (generally, premiums paid less prior withdrawals), (2) policy remains in force until death, (3) withdrawals taken during the first fifteen policy

here with tax benefits."

"So which one of the eleven doesn't fit into the insurance policy?" Michael asked.

"Guess," I challenged him.

"It's just like you to quiz me," Michael quipped.

"Try anyway."

"Okay. Tax-free withdrawals!"

"No. I'm sorry. Thanks for playing, though. The correct answer is one, the tax-deductible contributions." I plastered on the best game-show-host fake smile I could, eliciting a large grin from Michael.

I let my fake smile fade away and asked, "Now, are you ready to hear about the ten perfect investment characteristics?"

"Maybe you should read a little less of that IRS code book, okay?" he retorted.

"You know, I probably should."

"But you won't."

"No pain, no gain."

"Fair enough," Michael conceded, "as long as I'm one of those benefiting."

"You got it." We shook hands firmly as Big Mike smiled proudly.

---

years do not occur at the time of, or during the two years prior to, any reduction in benefits, and (4) the policy does not become a modified endowment contract. See IRC §§ 7702(f)(7)(B), 7702A. Any policy withdrawals, loans, and loan interest will reduce policy values and may reduce benefits.

CHAPTER 19
LOWER FEES
EQUALS MORE CASH

The secret is pure mathematics—put in the maximum amount of money and buy the minimum amount of life insurance death benefit allowable so you keep costs down and maintain the tax-deferral benefits.

In your later years, you can withdraw money tax free via the borrowing provision in your policy. You've now created a whole new vehicle to fund retirement strategies. The money you put into the policy after deducting expenses remains in your account.

How is the money invested? In this example, it is invested in an index universal life policy, the S&P 500 index without dividends, and it grows tax deferred with a floor of zero percent return on your investment. It's every investor's dream—an investment in which you take all of the up years and none of the down years.

To understand this concept better, let's draw a simple picture of what market volatility looks like. A few years ago, I read an article that stated the stock market produces a negative return on average one in every 3.45 years. That number is in constant flux, but you get the point: negative returns sabotage your positive gain years. It's like the old saying: "two steps forward and one step back."

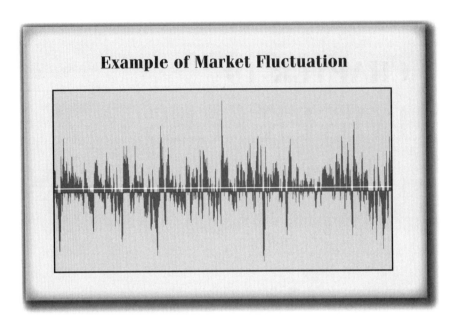

Example of Market Fluctuation

THE LOST DECADE (2000–2010)

Most people I know lost money over the ten-year period from 2000–2010. It appeared to be a wasted decade in terms of their financial lives, one that could never be replaced. The question is how many decades can be wasted before severely affecting a person's current and future lifestyles negatively?

If I could grant you one wish related to your annual investment returns, what would it be? You'd probably answer, "No more negative return years!"

Gee. Never lose money again. What a powerful concept!

This is what market volatility could look like with *no* down years:

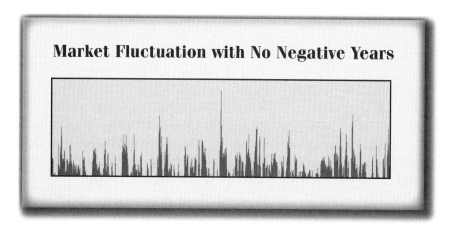

In this scenario, everyone can win the investment game.

Removes the downside pain and makes you feel a whole lot smarter, doesn't it?

TAX-FREE RETIREMENT DISTRIBUTIONS

Generally speaking, in these types of policies, any cash value within the policy after expenses accumulates tax deferred during the life of the policy. The policyholder may borrow from the life insurance policy's cash surrender value. Policyholders may borrow funds in the cash surrender value account at rates as low as one-quarter of 1 percent in the early years, and after year five years, many have a net zero borrowing cost. Yes, net zero—nothing, zilch.

Sounds pretty good when you compare it to mortgage financing at 5–7 percent, home equity loans at 6–8 percent, and credit cards at 29 percent, doesn't it?

Under IRC § 7702, policyholders borrow their own funds without paying taxes as long as the life insurance policy remains in force during the policyholder's lifetime.

The dollars grow—tax deferred throughout the life of the policy—and cash accumulating within the account can be withdrawn using the borrowing provision.

I pulled out a two-page presentation showing my brother Michael putting away $50,000 per year for twenty years—from his current age of thirty-one to age fifty-one—totaling $1 million.

At age sixty-six, based on the illustration showing the S&P index less dividends at 7 percent per year, he could withdraw $432,900 annually tax free until the age of eighty. So my brother puts in $1 million over twenty years and then he can withdraw $6,493,500 million tax free over fifteen years based on our example. That's a 6.4-to-1 tax-free return on his investment capital—and all the time his life insurance is still in place.

SAMPLE SUMMARY

Life Insurance Retirement Strategy Using Indexed Universal Life Insurance (Michael, Age 31)

PREMIUMS

Annual Premiums:	$50,000
Scheduled Years to Pay:	20
Total Premium Paid:	$1,000,000

DISTRIBUTIONS

Annual Distributions Age 66–80:	$432,900
Scheduled Years of Distributions:	15
Total Distributions:	$6,493,500

The only question at this point is, "What rate of return would Michael have to earn in a taxable investment to equal the tax-advantaged return with life insurance?"

Let's look at the recap I prepared for my brother.

SIMPLE MATHEMATICS FOR MICHAEL

I used simple math to show Michael that he could pay the premium in the policy once per year, combining the compelling tax-free benefits of the cash buildup inside a life insurance policy and the potential to profit from owning life insurance. As Big Mike said, "I don't see how not working and making almost half a million dollars a year at retirement can be bad!"

TAXABLE VERSUS TAX DEFERRAL

When you use life insurance and the accompanying benefits available to accumulate and withdraw tax-free cash, it is important to understand what rate of return is needed in a taxable investment to be equivalent. The following hypothetical example is used to illustrate my point.

Taxable Equivalent Return to Equal Tax Deferred Return

| | TAX RATE | | |
Tax Deferred	35%	30%	20%
5%	7.69%	7.14%	6.67%
6%	9.23%	8.57%	8.00%
7%	10.76%	10.00%	8.75%
8%	12.31%	11.42%	10.00%

In this example, you can see the power of tax benefits available. For example, if your tax deferred gross investment return this year is 7 percent, then you would have to earn 10.76 percent in the 35 percent tax rate to be equivalent. This is a hypothetical example and is not intended to be a projection of future values or performance.

Take a closer look at the tax efficiency of different assets, and you will see, in the graph below, the tax benefits in a properly designed life insurance policy. Basically, you are building a tax-advantaged haven in which your money will grow while you have access to those same appreciated assets without paying tax. Call it "Your Bank" or "Your Supplemental Retirement Plan." At the end of the day, it all means the same thing . . . tax efficient management of your money—and only life insurance provides a tax-free death benefit payoff when purchased correctly.

Investment Alternatives and Tax Efficiency

	Contribution Phase	Accumulation Phase	Distribution Phase
Certificate of Deposit	After Tax	Taxable	Nontaxable
Municipal Bonds	After Tax	Nontaxable*	Nontaxable*
Corporate Bonds	After Tax	Taxable	Taxable
Mutual Funds	After Tax	Taxable	Taxable
Qualified Pension Plans	Before Tax	Nontaxable	Taxable
Life Insurance Plans	**After Tax**	**Nontaxable**	**Nontaxable****

*Capital gains are taxed. Interest income is generally tax free.
**You may withdraw up to your basis tax free. Withdrawals beyond basis should be treated as loans and therefore not taxed unless the policy terminates. Many policies have net-zero cost loan provisions after a predetermined number of years. Loans do not have to be repaid based on policy performance.

CHAPTER 20

UP TO 1,000 PERCENT BETTER RETURNS FOR CHILDREN

Michael kept staring at the numbers. His face revealed an uncertainty about what to do next. I had never seen my brother—the genius in the family—quite this way.

Big Mike looked over at me, a smile on his face. He had always wanted to ensure that Michael would put away a chunk of money. He knew that without a plan and some assistance, Michael would put off doing so and might spend his money on things that didn't add any assets or value to his life beyond instant gratification. Big Mike knew, as did I, that the wheels were turning in Michael's head.

After a few moments, Michael lifted his eyes from the numbers before him and said, "Okay, I want to do this for myself, but let me ask a question. If overfunding the policy premiums each year and keeping the insurance costs down is the idea, would this work even better on my younger children?"

It was an intuitive question. Michaels's reasoning was extremely logical. If this plan worked this well for him, imagine what it could produce for his children.

Insurance costs are generally calculated based on your age, sex, and health rating. Generally speaking, the younger the person is, the lower the insurance costs. And that meant more cash accumulating in the account, tax deferred and compounding over twenty, thirty, forty years, or more!

"Let's see what the math looks like for a supplemental retirement plan, just like you ran for me, but this time for my children," Michael said. His children included William, who just turned two, and Robert, who was three.

Before I could run the numbers, Big Mike jumped in. He was having another moment of mathematical brilliance and just couldn't keep it to himself any longer. "You know, Michael, you and Brenda should just gift $12,000 per year per child. You would still be under the annual $13,000 exclusion, without any gift tax. Technically, you can gift up to $24,000 this year. That's $12,000 from you and $12,000 from your better half, Brenda, per year."

Big Mike was absolutely right. Why not gift $24,000 each year for the first sixteen years and withdraw $100,000 tax free to supplement college costs for years seventeen through twenty ($400,000 total)? After the boys finished college, Michael and Brenda could continue making annual gifts until they turned the policies over to their sons (once they were settled and secure in their careers). Ultimately, their sons could make the payments on the $24,000 per year premiums once they were established in their careers, and then withdraw the money tax free annually at retirement.

If they started out with a lower payment than $24,000, that would be okay because the annual premium amount can be flexible, with a range both up and down. The policy allowed that benefit, and they would just get less or more when they withdrew later. The structure could be designed for how small or large their commitment levels were.

"Michael, how excited do you think the children will be when they grow up and learn that they can flexibly pay in $24,000 annually for an estimated tax-free retirement income of almost $1 million per year over fifteen years?" I asked.

Michael laughed, ecstatic at the discovery of life insurance as an economic anchor for his family. "They'd go their entire lives without paying a penny in taxes on the cash in those policies—the spoiled brats."

I ran two illustrations. One showed the $24,000 in annual premiums through age sixty for Robert and William. The kids would each take a projected $400,000 out to cover college and then begin taking retirement money out for fifteen years, from ages sixty-six to eighty. The other option was to take out less, or more, when desired. Life insurance is flexible, just like an accordion—you can push or pull based on your needs and the performance of your money.

Let's recap the results for a supplemental retirement plan using investment-grade life insurance for Michael, age thirty-one, and his sons, Robert and William.

BENEFIT SUMMARY

Life Insurance Retirement Strategy Using Indexed Universal Life Insurance

PREMIUMS

	Michael, Age 31	Robert, Age 3	William, Age 2
Annual Premiums:	$50,000	$24,000	$24,000
Scheduled Years to Pay:	20	53	54
Total Premiums Paid:	$1,000,000	$1,272,000	$1,296,000

DISTRIBUTION

College Distributions (4 Years):	0.00	$400,000	$400,000
Annual Distributions (Ages 66–80):	$432,900	$808,230	$949,055
Scheduled Years of Distributions:	15	15	15
Total Distributions:	$6,493,500	$12,523,450	$14,635,825

INSURANCE BENEFITS

At Age 31:	$4,889,685	$2,520,453	$2,618,499
At Age 66:	$4,947,992	$2,858,189	$3,012,746
At Age 80:	$ 480,442	$1,023,796	$1,201,081

Working with your insurance professional: Review your current situation, considering your current income, net worth, existing insurance coverage, risk tolerance, time horizon, and current and projected liabilities. Outline your financial goals and objectives for you and your family for your lifetime and in the event of your death. Based on these factors, your life insurance professional can help you determine a life insurance strategy to help meet your insurance needs and financial objectives.

This material is not intended for use by any taxpayer for the purpose of avoiding US federal, state, or local tax penalties. This material is written to support the promotion or marketing of the transaction(s) or matter(s) addressed by this material. We do not provide tax, accounting, or legal advice. Any taxpayer should seek advice based on the taxpayer's particular circumstances from an independent tax advisor.

MICHAEL, AGE THIRTY-ONE

As you can see, age makes a substantial difference. At Michael's age of thirty-one, $50,000 per year over twenty years equals $1 million in total premiums. Retirement distributions beginning at age sixty-six are forecast at $432,900—8.6 times the annual premium.

That's $432,900 over fifteen years, which totals $6,493,500 in tax-free distributions. That's over six times the total premiums paid, plus the benefit of tax-free life insurance coverage for Brenda throughout Michael's entire life.

ROBERT, AGE THREE

Compare Roberts's policy, which begins at age three with $24,000 ($12,000 per spouse) per-year premiums through age sixty, with the exception of years seventeen through twenty, where no premiums are paid, but $100,000 per year is withdrawn tax free for college. A total of $1,272,000 in premiums will be paid through age sixty, and estimated tax-free withdrawals of $808,230 annually would begin at age sixty-six. The $808,230 would be withdrawn tax free for fifteen years, totaling $12,123,450. Add the $400,000 taken for college tax free, and the total projected tax-free withdrawal is $12,523,450.

That is 9.8 times the total premiums of $1,272,000!

WILLIAM, AGE TWO

Compare Robert's policy to William's policy, which begins at age two with $24,000 per year (premiums through age sixty with the exception of years seventeen through twenty, where no premiums are paid), but $100,000 per year withdrawn tax free for college. A total of $1,296,000 in premiums would be paid through age sixty and estimated tax-free withdrawals would begin at sixty-six at $949,055 annually. The $949,055 withdrawn tax free for fifteen years would total $14,235,825. Add the $400,000 taken for college tax free, and the total projected tax-free withdrawal is $14,635,825.

That is 11.2 times the total premiums of $1,296,000.

That's over $33 million in living wealth created over two generations with just over $3.5 million in premiums!

I put the "life" back in life insurance for Michael, Robert, and William! Investment-grade life insurance income: when no one dies, everyone wins and the money is enjoyed tax free during your lifetime!

Can you beat that? Really?

Didn't think so.

PART 5

DOUBLE
YOUR TAX-
ADVANTAGED
INCOME

CHAPTER 21

INCREASE YOUR INVESTMENT INCOME 100 PERCENT PLUS

One day, Big Mike called me and invited me to lunch. This may not seem to be something out of the ordinary for a father to do, but trust me, it was.

Big Mike usually didn't have time for lunch. His philosophy was that you never went out for lunch unless it was for new business. Therefore, he never left his office during lunch just to socialize That equated to ninety minutes of lost work time to him. I figured it must be something pretty important for him to leave his office before the close of the business day. I thought that perhaps he just wanted to talk more about his latest hobby, which I should probably more accurately describe as his obsession—helping me design and customize life insurance policies for our large family's various members.

Big Mike always knew that if he picked up the check for lunch, I was good for sharing one of the strategies I was working on. And, if he stuck around for dessert, I'd even flip open my "Idea Book" and explain the latest strategy I wanted to demonstrate mathematically, in a fundamentally new way.

He had already secured the best booth in his favorite Italian restaurant when I arrived. He greeted me with his arms wide open and the traditional Italian greeting—kissing both sides of my cheeks.

"You look good, David," he said. "Always so fit and healthy!"

"I'm living right, Dad. What can I say?"

"That's all you should say!" he exclaimed before insisting that I join him in the booth.

The waiter hurried over and poured a glass of red wine without even asking if I wanted it. Then I saw why. Big Mike was already readying his glass for a toast.

"To good news, good health, and good family," Big Mike said as he clinked his glass against mine.

He then savored the wine, stopping only when he noticed I was not drinking mine.

"Come on, David, we're celebrating!"

"Really?" I asked. "Well, maybe if you tell me what's worth celebrating—and why you are drinking before the workday is even half over—I'll join you."

Big Mike looked at me and smiled. "I'm having the best year in the business I've ever had, David!"

Well, there it was. A good reason to celebrate. I smiled and then knocked back a satisfying sip of the wine. Even with my ignorant palate, I could tell the full-bodied wine was an expensive one.

"I have no room to complain, do I?" Big Mike asked.

"No, you don't, Dad," I replied. "Besides, that's not what you're made of anyway."

He nodded in agreement.

"So, Dad," I continued. "What can I do for you?"

Big Mike then spilled the reason for this impromptu lunch. "One of my top engineers, Pete Downs, came to see me the other day, seeking advice for his mother's investment portfolio. Her name is Eva, and she just turned eighty, though she sounds like she has the energy of a woman half her age. She just returned from a hiking trip at Glacier National Park in Montana."

I knew the area well. It was just north of Whitefish, where my friend Randy owned a home on the lake.

Big Mike continued with his story. "Eva is a widow with $1 million. She lives off the income it produces. The problem is she started out with $2 million just before the crash in 2007, when her husband passed. The market crash turned that $2 million into $1 million really fast, and her panic reaction was to move the money to cash, so she had no chance to make any of it back on the market rebound. Now, she has sworn off risk, and her money is parked in short-term bonds, where she earns an average of just 3 percent per year after taxes. She is scared to death about making another mistake. The $30,000 per year is not much to live on, even for a woman with no debt except her small mortgage."

Big Mike was talking quickly, trying to get it all out. "David, I'm motivated to help her. Please help me find a safe and secure strategy to increase her income. And just so you know—just to make your job a little more difficult—she has promised her three children a nice little inheritance when she passes. Can't we—I mean, you—find out what the best alternative would be for her to move her money, increase her income, and have enough left over to leave a small legacy with her children? You know, just like you've taught me to do in the life insurance industry?"

I turned to Big Mike and asked a simple question: "Dad, if I understand you correctly, you just want me to handle this quickly and simply, right?"

"Yes, nothing complicated at all. I'm counting on you!" he said, and I could see him relax as the pressure to help Pete find a solution to his mother's challenging financial situation was transferred to me.

CHAPTER 22

FREE CHEESE FROM THE MOON

Imagine for a minute that I am handing you a magic wand while asking you the following question: "If you could waive this magic wand and grant yourself two wishes, as an investor, what two wishes would they be—within reason, of course?"

You'd most likely answer with the following. "I never want a negative return again—all positive and *no* negatives." And, "I want an above-average return for the risk I am taking."

Isn't that what we all want? All ups and no downs and above-average, tax-advantaged income annually?

Sure it is. But is that even possible? You might as well grant yourself more wishes: income for life, predictability, and a $1 million tax-free bonus for the kids.

If you believe in all that, then you would probably believe that we can drink wine as we nibble on little cheese slices from the moon.

But the fact is . . . it's all true.

TO PROVE A POINT—CHEESE AND ALL

Let's look at Eva's predicament. She has a finite amount of cash to live on, and that amount just decreased from $2 million to $1 million in the last few years. She is scared of the negative change in lifestyle while she's still adjusting to the $1 million loss. Her cash invested currently is earning a net, after tax and fees, of 3 percent, or $30,000 per year. As I said previously, $30,000 per year is not much to live on, even for a woman with no debt (except for a $1,000 per month payment on a house that will be paid off in five years).

Total it all up, and you have $12,000 in annual mortgage payments and only $18,000 remaining, or $1,500 per month. That may be okay for a healthy eighty-year-old who doesn't leave her neighborhood, but Eva is an active and vivacious eighty-year-old who likes to travel.

I called Big Mike after I had put together the solution, and we agreed to meet for a quick lunch at Santapio's Pizza.

"So, have you come up with the solution to Eva's problem?" he asked as we settled into a booth in the restaurant. I told him to sit back and relax. I had indeed found a solution to the problem.

I asked Big Mike if he thought a 100-percent-plus guaranteed raise for Eva, 95 percent tax-free distributions for years one through ten, and a $1 million tax-free bonus for the kids to split would be worth thirty minutes of her time.

THE IMMEDIATE ANNUITY INCOME & INVESTMENT DOUBLER

I explained to Big Mike that an immediate life annuity could be just the solution for Eva. With it, Eva would give the life insurance company a check for $1 million. In return, the life insurance company would provide Eva with a guaranteed stream of income paid monthly, or annually, for the rest of her life. You see, the older you are, the more the insurance company pays you, because your life expectancy is shorter.

In this case, I received offers from ten different companies. The best offer was $105,396 per year. That equates to 3.5 times higher than the $30,000 Eva was currently receiving. Now at first glance, the $105,396 appeared to be a 10.5 percent payout for the rest of her life. Even better, for the first ten years, 94.9 percent of the distributions would not be taxable because they were a return of her basis. That's why it's technically called an annuity payout amount and not a 10.5 percent return. Her net after tax during those early years would be $103,891, and in the later years, $75,885. Those numbers are estimated at her 28 percent tax rate based on current tax law.

With an assumed average life expectancy of eleven years, the breakeven on Eva's $1 million investment is just under ten years. The critical piece is the following: if Eva selected the "life guarantee" option to get the highest payout annually, it would mean that when Eva died, the life insurance company would keep whatever was left, if any, of her $1 million.

Big Mike shook his head from side to side, a terrible look of confusion spreading across his face. He had been following me up until the last part where the insurance company would keep Eva's money if she died earlier than expected. I prepared myself for the question I knew was coming.

"What kind of risk are you asking Eva to take?" he asked. If she dies in year four, she would have only received $420,000 out of her $1 million, and her kids get *nothing*! She is out almost $600,000! You can't be serious, David, can you?"

I was. Here's why.

The $103,891 net Eva would receive in years one through ten was $73,891 higher annually than the $30,000 she was currently receiving. So . . .

- If we increase her payout from $30,000 to $73,891, or 100 percent plus, that would leave $50,000 to fund the children's inheritance.
- Eva would gift the $50,000 annually into an irrevocable life insurance trust (ILIT), using a portion of her $13,000 annual gift per person maximum for the benefit of her four children. Four children times $13,000 equals $52,000, the maximum she can gift per year. Since she is putting only $50,000 per year in the ILIT, she is $2,000 under the maximum amount, and she will pay no gift tax.
- The trust would purchase a $1 million life insurance policy on Eva for $50,000 in annual premiums for the benefit of the four children.

- At her death, whether it was four years or fourteen years, the life insurance company would pay the $1 million death benefit income- and estate-tax free to the trust.

- The trust would divide the assets equally between the children and pay them, per the trust documents, $250,000 each, tax free.

Win. Win. Win.

With such a policy, Eva could stop worrying and start living without the stress of market and income fluctuations—while creating a tax-free legacy for her family.

There are many forms of this strategy, some with death benefits and some without, just like the one above. Remember, you cannot outlive your income.

So just look at what we accomplished for Eva:

1. Provided an enhanced income stream, beginning at $103,891 a year in years one through ten, that is guaranteed by the insurance company. Then Eva gifted $50,000 to her children, who bought a $1 million life insurance policy on Eva.

2. Allowed her to receive tax-advantaged income.

3. Replaced nonperforming and underperforming assets.

4. Removed an asset from Eva's estate for tax purposes and increased her income.

5. Left a legacy of $1 million for her children.

6. Delivered two products, neither of which are correlated to any of the traditional real estate, stock, or bond markets.

Big Mike looked at me skeptically, stopping me cold, and then a smile began to form at the corners of his mouth. "I am so proud to know what you have presented will change the quality of life for Eva—and for many others, for the rest of their lives."

Big Mike's gratitude was genuine. "Thank you, Dad," I responded. "How you feel right now is how I feel when I help people succeed at the highest level. It's the real reason I came into this business in the first place."

I then asked Big Mike two questions:

1. How many people do you know who have underperforming assets in their portfolios?
2. How many people do you know who have lost money at least twice within the last ten years?

Big Mike groaned. "Everyone I know. And now I get the point. But how would they ever know unless they met you or someone like you who knows?"

True enough. I went on to explain that there are different products used for different ages. For example, with younger people, there are guaranteed annual income account values that credit one's account from 6–8 percent annually, and seniors can access products with payouts from 7–15 percent on average.

This exercise in finding the right policy for Eva reminded me of the similarities between the life insurance business and sports. Sports taught me the value of great coaching. Frank Serrao, who coached the football team on which Grandpa Fred played at the University of Redlands, was such a coach. He built winning teams on the strength of young men who were taught to have great character. You see, the true character of a person comes out when he or she is under the most stress. And the difference between a good team and a great team is more than the number of individual All-Americans, more than developing a habit of winning—it's getting the best out of each player under those stressful situations. It is all about how you finish—and that means winning championships.

The same can be true about the business world. When I started my career, I wanted to be coached by the best. I wanted to learn how to get the best financial results for my clients, and I knew that finding a winning coach with a winning track record would make the odds of winning go sky high for my clients and me.

At the end of the day, the difference between good and great is a fraction of inch.

PART 6

SAVE UP TO 65 PERCENT IN TAXES ON PENSION ASSETS

CHAPTER 23

MULTIPLY PENSION MONEY TEN TIMES

There's a certain sense of accomplishment you carry when you help someone who is feeling desperate and stressed. Big Mike certainly felt it. I could tell by the smile that beamed on his face in the weeks after we had helped Eva. In some small way, Big Mike and I had been fortunate to short circuit Eva's pending disaster and provide her with a sense of security and the feeling that she was on top of the world once again.

In the weeks that followed our final meeting with Eva and her son Pete, Big Mike had mentioned a potential tax problem with his $2 million pension plan. He had been concerned about the most efficient strategy to get his money out of the plan while legitimately paying the least amount of tax.

After reviewing the plan, I had sent him a recap on the magnitude of the $1.4 million tax problem I had calculated, as well as a possible solution I called "pension rescue." He had replied with a three-word e-mail: "See you Sunday." I understood the brevity of the message. Big Mike did not like surprises, and I knew the multimillion problem I had outlined for him was a jolt to his system.

That Sunday, I went over to his house. From the looks of him, you would've thought that Big Mike had seen a ghost. He was shaken, and my brothers and I knew it. We took our places at the table, waiting for him to speak. The air was so thick we could have cut it with a knife. My only hope was that the conversation would end on a happier note than the one on which it was starting.

Big Mike looked directly at me. I knew that what was bothering him was my pension rescue strategy. You see, Big Mike had a success problem. He was so successful at putting pretax money into his pension plan that he had run into one of his biggest success problems to date—he faced up to 65 percent tax getting the money out of the plan!

Big Mike could not get over the fact that his qualified pension plan had been a great accumulation vehicle, but one of the worst-taxed distribution vehicles. So I explained to Big Mike some of the pluses and minuses of fully funding qualified retirement plans.

ESTATE TAX PROBLEM

If Big Mike and Mom both died, the $2 million would turn into approximately $780,000, up to a 65 percent reduction. That's after the 35 percent estate tax *and* up to 40 percent combined income tax on the remainder. That is:

- $2 million minus the 35 percent estate tax equals $1.3 million.
- $1.3 million minus the estimated 40 percent combined income tax equals $520,000, leaving an estimated $780,000 to heirs.

DISTRIBUTION PROBLEM

The second problem began when the distributions began. Distributions from age fifty-nine and a half onward are taxed at the current federal and state income tax, which is approximately 40 percent. The problem was exacerbated because Big Mike wanted his money in one big lump sum. That is:

- Big Mike's contributions grew to $2 million at age seventy.
- If Big Mike had closed the plan and distributed the entire $2 million at age seventy, *he would have paid approximately $800,000 in income taxes* and taken home approximately $1.2 million. That would have been a 40 percent reduction.

Big Mike had just turned seventy and realized his $2 million was in "tax jail" and he could not get to it without paying an $800,000 ransom. I guess in the back of his mind he had always known he would have to pay taxes when he withdrew the money. The problem was that when it came time to write a check for that amount, he realized he should have listened to me over the years (although he would never admit that). He should have done some planning and not waited until the horse was out of the corral, so to speak.

He was not happy. "If I'm so smart, how come no one told me at retirement I was going to turn $2 million into $1.2 million after taxes—or worse, that my children would only receive approximately $780,000 after estate and income taxes if Mom and I both passed away while the money is still in the plan?"

THE SIMPLE, LITTLE-KNOWN SOLUTION

I asked Big Mike if he really needed the money from the pension plan to live on. After all, his business was projected to do over $100 million in annual sales in a down economy. With a 15 percent bottom-line net profit, that was real money we were talking about.

I explained the obvious need for tax planning to get his pension money out of tax jail at the least possible cost.

So I asked the key question again: "Do you really need the pension distribution money to live on?"

He shook his head no and replied, "The objective was to grow the pension money as large as possible with the least amount of risk and tax bite, and then pass it on to the grandkids."

I smiled. That was all I needed to hear. The plan I had for Big Mike would allow the grandkids to hit the jackpot without ever having to go to Vegas.

I unveiled my plan, giving Big Mike the worst options first. He had two choices: He could keep his plan in place, take annual distributions of $117,000, and pay the combined income tax estimated at $51,500, netting him $65,500, or he could terminate the plan and pay the $800,000 lump sum tax. Obviously, there are no clear victories with these two options.

IT GETS WORSE

Of course, it would be worse if he were to take the annual distributions and not fund the gifts to pay the life insurance premiums. Why?

Well, if Big Mike were to take the annual distributions and then he and Mom died in an accident, in the fifth year, the remaining assets in the pension plan would be subject to an estate tax of up to 35 percent, as well as federal and state income taxes estimated at 40 percent of the remainder.

That would total up to 65 percent, or $1,220,000 in taxes on the entire $2 million pension plan.

That would net the grandchildren just $780,000 out of $2 million, or $60,000 each.

Do you think that was Big Mike's original intention for his $2 million?

Absolutely not!

THE NET-ZERO COST STRATEGY

The plan I presented to Big Mike was elegant in its simplicity.

Using the pension plan, Big Mike would begin taking the required minimum distributions from the plan at age seventy and a half and purchase a second-to-die life insurance policy (on Big Mike and Mom that pays off at the second death).

Big Mike agreed to this, and using the pension plan assets, he began taking annual distributions from his plan, paid the income tax, and then gifted the net after-tax distribution of $65,500 to an irrevocable life insurance trust (ILIT) with the twelve grandchildren as beneficiaries.

The idea is simple. The trustee, who is my uncle Mike in Colorado, purchases a second-to-die life insurance policy whose annual premiums equal the annual gift to the trust of $65,500. Each and every year thereafter, Big Mike takes a distribution from the plan, pays the income tax, and gifts the $65,500 remainder to the trust to fund the life insurance premium for the grandchildren.

That would buy $6 million of life insurance based on their health and their ages (seventy for Big Mike and sixty for Mom), which is ninety-two times the annual premium of $65,500. The annual premium is just $65,500, or just shy of 1.1 percent of the death benefit of $6 million.

That was a whole lot better than any of the other devastating options above.

TEN TIMES MORE MONEY TAX FREE

Big Mike and Mom turned a $2 million pension asset tied up in tax jail into $6 million, estate- and income-tax free for the grandkids. Think about it. That's NO TAXES down two generations from Big Mike and Mom to the twelve grandchildren.

So what was our new worst-case scenario? Even if Mom and Dad passed away suddenly—after making the first-year $65,500 premium gift to the trust and the trustee's paying the first premium—the $2 million pension plan suffers the worst consequences of estate and income tax, leaving an estimated $780,000 to the grandkids. On the other hand, the one and only, net-after-tax, $65,500 premium they gifted to the trust from the pension distribution bought a $6 million death benefit that pays the children $6 million income- and estate-tax free. Wow! That is $500,000 per child.

Big Mike and Mom figured that my brothers and I had enough money coming from their estate, so they wanted to set up something specifically for the grandchildren to remember them by.

IN CONCLUSION

The $6 million equates to $500,000 per child, which is over seven times better than the worst-case scenario of netting $780,000, or $65,000 per child, if Big Mike and Mom passed away suddenly with the money still in the pension plan.

If you never ask, you never get. If you ask and you get, you keep asking.

PART 7

PAY ZERO ESTATE TAX AND DOUBLE THE SIZE OF YOUR ESTATE

CHAPTER 24

"PRECIOUS CARGO"

When my daughter Ava was born, my wife Carrie went on a mission to find the safest, coolest, most fuel-efficient compact sport SUV in the state.

It took her all of twenty minutes, thanks to the Internet. Less than an hour later, I attached my John Hancock to the contract, and we had our very own four-wheeled family fortress.

Any doubt in buying the vehicle had been quickly removed when I saw Carrie look at our sleeping daughter and then whisper "precious cargo."

Like me, you have your own precious cargo.

Everyone has good intentions. Everyone hopes to provide better lives for his or her family. But how many of us can actually guarantee that our family's financial future is secure?

Have you ever thought about leaving a family legacy for generations to come—maybe even set up a charitable family foundation with your heirs employed and administering the direction of the annual gifts?

If you have, you should know by now that it's possible.

The only thing that might be holding you back from establishing one is the absence of a sound strategy and some planning—and the right help.

And that is exactly why I wrote this book—to open your mind to what's truly possible and genuinely real. When you understand the math behind the strategies, you'll truly understand one of the most misunderstood but effective methods to multiply family wealth.

I urge those who want their hard-earned money to start working for them to consider investment-grade life insurance. It's the best financial vehicle that's come along in the last 100 years. Because the math makes sense, you know the returns are real—not just real, but if designed properly, they can be spectacular and even income- and estate-tax free.

Protect your own generations of precious cargo. I know I've protected mine.

CHAPTER 25

GIVE YOUR ESTATE AWAY TWICE

Big Mike's seventieth birthday party was a big hit. The entire family gathered at Pasquale's Italian Restaurant for cocktails and left only when the bar closed its doors in the wee hours of the morning. In retrospect, we should've just rented out the restaurant for the evening because we took up almost every table inside.

My proud and smiling father was surrounded by almost every person he loved and cared about—his family, friends, and business associates (a virtual Who's Who of leading businessmen and state politicians). There was the typical playful family banter and the epic, exaggerated stories—all followed by the inevitable hysterical laughter from everyone.

The night was, quite simply, perfect.

My brothers and I just sat back and enjoyed the special moment, listening to everyone relate how his or her life had been touched by Big Mike.

We were profoundly humbled and truly surprised to hear the amazing stories of his quiet mentoring of lifelong family friends. We learned how he had taught them to be successful and had never asked for or accepted a dime in return. They were his friends, he said, and they would've done the same thing for him had he needed it. We knew otherwise. Few people could have ever helped him as unselfishly as he had helped others achieve their dreams.

The weekend after his birthday party, we all gathered for our traditional Sunday night family dinner. We discovered that Big Mike had been thinking long and hard about his legacy. He joked that he was in the "fourth quarter" of the metaphorical football game of life, and one day the game would go on without him. It was not something I wanted to hear. I couldn't imagine my life without the leadership and wise counsel of Big Mike.

However, like the true leader he was, Big Mike shepherded the adults into the living room and, once we were all seated and attentive, asked us all to consider who we really were as a family.

What did we stand for? How did we want to be remembered?

"I've never been happier in my life," he began. "And I owe much of that—if not all of it—to all of you. From the bottom of my heart, I thank you for the best birthday party I've ever had. Special thanks to all of you for sharing so many amazing stories that I now realize define my life. It's really the first time that I've reflected on the journey. I was always so busy thinking about the future and providing for it that I had not thought much about our shared past. I honestly had no idea I had made such an impression on so many people, and I am forever humbled by your kind words and fond memories."

This was an emotional Big Mike, one we had seldom seen growing up. I think that since the birthday party, he had finally slowed down long enough to reflect on just how much of an impact he'd had on the course and direction of so many lives—his wife, his four sons and their wives, his twelve grandchildren, the 150 employees whom he insisted on treating as part of the family, as well as the countless friends and relatives who had come into his life.

And now, Big Mike was acknowledging his own mortality. He paused for what seemed like an eternity, wiped away some tears that had escaped from his eyes, and said, "I realize now, more than I ever have before, just how important it is to build a lasting and enduring family legacy for future generations." He walked over to the window and pulled aside the drape, revealing the grandchildren happily at play outside. "So that they may have the same opportunities to grow and prosper as we all did."

He turned back to face us. "After a lot of thought and discussion, your Mom and I have decided to follow a very simple plan that will leave a legacy for everyone who wants to participate. Our family estate legacy is valued at $100 million after all exemptions for estate-tax planning purposes. We expect you, as stewards of this money, to grow it and use it wisely so that future generations may inherit even more. It is our fervent hope, and our only request, that you do not diminish the funds you will each receive."

The goal in this planning process is to get as much money to my brothers and me as possible. The $100 million is subject to estate taxes—estimated 35 percent—leaving $35 million in estate taxes due upon their deaths.

The remaining $65 million would go to my brothers and me.

Big Mike then shared with us how he was going to give away the family's assets twice without incurring any estate taxes.

"The strategy is so simple that I don't need say it more than once. We'll turn $65 million of what you would have received after estate taxes when we are gone into $182 million. The brilliance of the strategy I've gone over with David is simple: Mom and I are going to take $18 million of the $100 million and, working with a tax attorney, set it up to allow you boys to buy a $100 million life insurance policy on both of our lives using the $18 million to pay for the policy. That will reduce the size of our taxable estate from $100 million to $82 million. After Mom and I both pass away, the estimated $82 million, which will represent our entire estate, will be gifted to a qualified charity and not subject to estate tax."

Big Mike smiled. "The $100 million payoff from the life insurance policy, which will be owned outside of our estate by you boys for tax purposes, will be divided equally so each of you boys receives $25 million income- and estate-tax free. There is obviously more strategy and detail behind the scenes, but generally speaking, it's really as smooth as it sounds."

My brothers and their wives just sat there, stunned. Big Mike and I had come up with a win-win plan, in which my three brothers and I would equally split $100 million, and the charities would receive approximately $82 million. That was a total of $182 million—a big leap from splitting $65 million with no charitable gift!

Remember: The person who understands the math controls the deal. Protect your own generations of precious cargo!

It's really just this simple.

CHAPTER 26

TURN $65 MILLION INTO $182 MILLION

Big Mike was always three or four steps ahead—and the brilliance of his and Mom's decision to "keep life simple" and solve their estate tax and legacy planning in one fell swoop fit their personalities perfectly. However, I have to be honest. There was a little bump in the road in getting to this point.

While I had exposed Big Mike and Mom to some very high-level planning techniques from some of the best tax and legal minds in the industry, it had all come to a crashing halt during one particular meeting I will never forget.

Two weeks before the big announcement, Big Mike and I had driven into Boston for one more legacy-planning strategy. The meeting had been with Arthur Greenberg, a top tax attorney, regarding legacy planning, estate planning, asset protection, and business succession planning, among other things. It had started well, but the more we talked, the more complicated everything seemed to become—until a friendly discussion finally turned into a heated argument.

Phrases like *estate-tax portability, possible reunification of the gift- and estate-tax exemption, charitable lead trusts, grantor-retained annuity trusts, installment sale to an intentionally defective trust* (IDIT sale) and *enhanced generation-skipping transfer tax plan*—they had confused Big Mike and made his head spin (even though they were all effective alternatives that had worked for many of my clients in one form or another). But what had finally pushed him over the edge was when he heard that the government could pass legislation changing the carefully planned strategies we had designed. That was it for Big Mike. The meeting was over.

Big Mike thanked everyone and then headed to the car without saying a word. He wasn't talking or even thinking about making a decision regarding any of it. It was so unlike him to freeze up. I didn't know how to respond.

On the way home, I got Big Mike to agree to stop for a lobster roll at Kelly's, the famous local eatery that produces some of the finest fried clams, seafood, and lobster rolls anywhere in the world. I thought this would give me an opportunity to get Big Mike to open up. So we ordered our takeout and then sat together on a bench near the beach across the street from Kelly's.

After a while, Big Mike started to calm down. We enjoyed some small talk until I grabbed the floor and took the opportunity to put everything about the meeting back into perspective. Legacy planning, I told him, should ultimately be fun, something he obviously was not having at the moment.

I looked directly at him and asked, "Dad, if I told you that you just lost $35 million dollars and that your $100 million estate was now worth $65 million, what would your initial reaction be?"

Big Mike responded, "That would be devastating, and I know that is what's going to happen if I don't do any planning."

I waited until that sank in for both of us and continued: "Dad, if I could show you how to turn that $35 million loss into $182 million tax free, would you give me a few more minutes?"

I saw the flicker of hope come back into Big Mike's eyes. He waved me on with those prizefighter-sized hands of his.

"Okay, just play along with me here—just think outside the box for a moment so we can see if there is a solution," I said. "What if the IRS sent you a letter like the following?"

I paused, for effect, and then quickly made up a fictitious missive.

Dear Taxpayer:

*We have been informed that upon your death and that of your wife, your heirs will owe the United States Government the sum of **$35,000,000** in death taxes. These taxes are payable in cash or by money order within **nine months** of the last demise.*

Payment can be made by liquidating assets of your estate or from cash which you have already paid taxes on and saved for your family. If you don't like these two options, we have two creative strategies using life insurance detailed in Option A or Option B below.

Option A:

*We offer an alternative installment plan for selected taxpayers. Your current taxable estate is valued at $100,000,000 after all exemptions, so this would require a one-time payment of **$6,500,000**, which represents 6.5 percent of your $100,000,000 taxable estate if paid now. (You may also opt for annual payments.) After making this $6,500,000 payment, we would consider your taxes "PAID IN FULL", as this $6,500,000 will buy a one-pay life insurance policy on you and your wife totaling $35,000,000, which is exactly the amount you will owe. That equates to an 82 percent discount.*

Option B:

*This option would require a one-time payment of **$18,000,000**, which represents just 18 percent of your $100,000,000 taxable estate if paid now. (You may also opt for annual payments). This 18,000,000 will buy a one-pay life insurance policy on you and your wife totaling $100,000,000. This policy, similar to Option A, can be purchased by your children with* *cash you will provide through any number of estate-planning strategies. Your children will be the beneficiaries, so the proceeds will be received income- and estate-tax free.*

*That would leave **$82,000,000** in your estate and your children would hold the $100,000,000 life insurance policy outside of your estate. Now this strategy is simple: Have the entire $82,000,000 gifted to a qualified charity upon your death. At the same time, the life insurance company would pay your children the life insurance benefit of $100,000,000 income- and estate-tax free.*

We would consider your taxes "PAID IN FULL," as there is "no tax." In effect, you would have turned your $100 million estate, which was destined to become $65 million at your death, into an $182,000,000 estate, delivered a legacy to your family, and made the impossible possible for a few very happy charitable institutions.

Should you desire to explore this matter further, the agent bearing this letter can explain more fully how this attractive life insurance arrangement works.

I remain your "Favorite Uncle."

Very truly yours,

UNCLE SAM

As "Uncle Sam" dribbled out of my mouth, Big Mike straightened up and belted out, "OPTION B! Let's not waste another week! Put everything together so we cross every 't' and dot every 'i.' Let's meet once more to flush out all the details with my attorney, and then plan to announce the news to our family in a few weeks!"

And that's the full story behind Big Mike's emotional night when he broke the news to the family that he was giving his estate away twice.

As I referenced above, there are a lot a sound strategies to handle tax, legacy, and estate planning. For most clients, it's like trying to learn a new language in only three two-hour meetings before you sign the final documents that ultimately affect almost everything you have or own. This process entails placing a large amount of trust in professionals whom they hardly know.

Most successful people I know are used to being in control, not out of control, and a crash course on who is going to get their money is not an exciting proposition. The stark reality is that losing 35 percent of your money—or as in Big Mike's case, $35 million—and realizing that the government became your silent 65/35 partner as soon as you crossed the threshold to success is a major problem that deserves a viable solution.

The idea of this chapter has been to get you to open your mind to intriguing, yet brilliantly simple, possibilities. The more traditional estate-tax-planning strategy is noted below. Just remember that everyone is different and professional advisors can show you all of your options. The more money you have, the more options you have based on your own situation.

MY "FOR-PROFIT" STRATEGY

I recommend families buy second-to-die survivorship policies to profit the next generation or two and even your favorite charities. Why? Because of the lower cost of annual premiums on two lives versus one life. Diversify your investment portfolio and include the purchase of life insurance for as much or as little as you want to accomplish in tax-free cash. It just makes sound financial sense.

If you cannot spend all your money in your lifetime, what you learned here is that mathematically you can give a whole lot more away in a tax-efficient manner with life insurance strategies than leaving your money invested in your name until you pass. It just makes sense to take advantage of the benefits offered from the life insurance companies and the corresponding tax benefits that are available to you.

MORE TRADITIONAL ESTATE-TAX-REDUCTION STRATEGY PROBLEM

More traditional estate-tax-reduction strategies would work like this: Big Mike and Mom have a $100 million taxable estate and an approximate 35 percent estate tax looming in the future when the second one of them dies. This tax due would reduce the $100 million taxable estate to $65 million.

SOLUTION

My parents would strategically move $6.5 million out of the estate to a trust for the benefit of the four boys through a variety of planning strategies, and the boys would buy a one-pay $35 million second-to-die life insurance policy on Big Mike and Mom.

The premiums could also be funded through annual gifts, and the life insurance policy premiums could be broken out and paid annually instead of in one lump payment. A one-pay premium generally happens to be the cheapest method of payment.

Upon the second death, the trust would receive the $35 million payoff from the life insurance company, income- and estate-tax free and, in turn, pay the government the $35 million estate tax. The children would take possession of the entire $100 million in family assets in the estate, including the home, real estate, businesses, and securities.

BENEFIT

The $35 million estate tax would be discounted 82 percent to $6.5 million because, in effect, the $6.5 million premium bought the $35 million policy that paid the IRS. That's a $28.5 million savings. The alternative without the $35 million of tax-free life insurance would be the forced liquidation of assets by the brothers to satisfy the $35 million tax at whatever price the heirs could fetch in the current market.

CHAPTER 27
NOW IT'S YOUR TURN

I'll let you in on a secret . . . well, two actually.

The journey you just took with Big Mike and his fictitious family was not entirely fictitious at all. That's my real family, which includes Big Mike, Mom, and my brothers Michael, John, and Tom. I took some liberties on each family member's character description. This is a real family wrapped into a fictional story that is based on real-life insurance strategies that generated over $170 million in additional net worth.

How did it happen to us? Well, that's the second secret. It's what I call the secret asset—investment-grade life insurance.

Most people cannot fully grasp how investment-grade life insurance can create incredible wealth for families. Can learning about all the options be confusing? Yes. Can it be overwhelming? Yes. But with the right attitude, the right strategies, and the right financial help, you can win—and win big. You can create a legacy for your own precious cargo.

So now you know my story. What are you waiting for?

Now it's your turn. I'm going to help you take the first step. You and I are going to remove the first roadblock that is preventing you from starting one of the most lucrative financial undertakings of your lifetime.

So let's have a big whine and list all the reasons why we shouldn't do anything.

Ready? Here we go.

- I'm too old.
- My husband would never qualify.
- My wife would never qualify.
- I'm divorced.
- We don't have time.
- My kids are going to get enough money anyway.
- Why spoil them?
- I don't have enough money.
- My situation is already handled.
- My cousin handles my insurance.
- I had a bad experience twenty years ago.
- I'll make enough money to solve it.
- My dog died.
- My cat ran away.

Let's get serious. We are talking about real money here. Life insurance can pay off in cash both during your life and after you are gone, depending on exactly what you want to achieve.

In this story alone, you have seen how

- We made $12 million for Big Mike's parents;
- We used the $1.3 million cash in the policy on Mom's parents to generate a future gift of $12 million to the University of Redlands;
- We helped my brother Michael and his children generate over $33

million in estimated tax-free income for a little over $3.5 million;

- We turned Eva's $1 million into $2 million after doubling her annual income;

- We created Big Mike's pension rescue strategy, which generated $12 million; and

- We turned Big Mike and Mom's estimated $65 million estate after tax into a $182 million tax-free windfall.

Add it all up, and our family generated over $170 million in new cash—with a secret asset called investment-grade life insurance.

The next step is up to you. Imagine what your money tree could look like when you replace my family with your own.

You can win . . . again and again and again.

Just look at the math specific to your situation, and you can make a well-informed business decision. You have absolutely nothing to lose.

Take care of your precious cargo. It's really that simple.

|ABOUT THE AUTHOR

David D'Arcangelo is a recognized author, speaker, and insurance expert who has spent almost three decades helping people achieve financial success.

A master financial strategist, he has performed at both corporate and national events, sharing the stage with such well-known speakers such as Zig Ziglar, Mark Victor Hansen, Anthony Robbins, Barbara Bush, and General Norman Schwarzkopf.

David is the former host of the TV show *Money Talk* on the PRIMESTAR satellite network's TPN channel. His published books and programs include *The 49 Hottest Home-Based Business Tax Strategies*, *Wealth Talk*, *Money Smart*, and his most recent book, *Wealth Starts at Home,* published by McGraw-Hill.

In 1990, David cofounded The Financial Destiny Companies with Anthony Robbins. He later went on to serve as chairman and founder of Entreport Corporation and as president and director of AMS Health Sciences, Inc., both of which were listed on the American Stock Exchange.

Currently, David is president of The D'Arcangelo Companies, a diversified company delivering business marketing, training, and consulting services. The D'Arcangelo Companies is an industry innovator working in combination with life insurance agents internationally to provide superior strategies and insurance products for individuals, affluent families, and business owners.

David received a BA in economics/business administration from the University of Redlands, where he was a former All-American football player and inductee into the university's hall of fame. He currently resides in Solana Beach, California, with his wife, Carrie; daughter, Ava Bella; and their three beagles, Tina, Sammy, and Rascal—although he remains true to his Boston roots by continuing to be a die-hard fan of the Boston Celtics, Boston Bruins, Boston Red Sox, and New England Patriots.